# WHY
## Do You Believe In
# GOD?

Catholic Conversations with Skeptics
and Non-Believers

Bryan Mercier

## DEDICATION:

To the Lord Jesus with love and thanksgiving! For all of Your sheep that they may hear Your voice and find abundant life in You!

## ACKNOWLEDGEMENTS:

First and foremost, I would like to thank my most beautiful wife Katherine for her constant prayer and support in all of my ministry work including this book and for all her work in helping to design the cover. Thanks my love!

Second, I would like offer a huge thank you to Libby Reichert for all the time and invaluable help she generously offered. This book would not be what it is without her help. Lastly, I would like to extend a big thank you to Myriah Boudreaux, Carrie O'Connell, Katie Eads, and everyone else who helped make this book possible.

THANK YOU!

# Table of Contents:

# The Purpose Of This Book

*Questions!* Everybody has questions about God, religion, faith, and the meaning of life. Unfortunately, we do not always receive satisfying answers to our questions. Too many times the phrases "just have faith" or "it's a mystery" are tossed around carelessly. However, non-answers like this do not usually bring anyone closer to God and will probably push them further away.

The purpose of this book is twofold. First, it is intended to give real answers to the good questions people have regarding God and questions of faith. Secondly, it seeks to serve as an apologetics[1] handbook. It will offer the arguments and objections that skeptics have against God and the Catholic religion while demonstrating how to effectively answer them. It will also help Christians to become more confident and proficient in sharing their faith with others.

The stories in this book are actual conversations that the author has had.[2] The conversation format of this book will make reading easier and learning more interesting. Our hope

---

[1] Apologetics is the study of learning how to defend and explain your faith to others in a convincing manner.

[2] Some parts of this book may have been altered a bit for grammatical reasons, for the sake of clarity, to protect people's identity, or for apologetics purposes.

is that people who are searching will find the answers they are looking for and that people of faith will be set on fire and become more adept in explaining their beliefs.

# Introductory Notes From The Author

Note #1: There is a distinction between atheist, agnostic, and skeptic. An atheist is a person who absolutely does not believe in God. An agnostic is someone who is undecided or unsure on the question but is open to the possibility of a higher power. A skeptic is a person who has doubts about God, the spiritual life, or different aspects of religion in general. Skeptics can be believers or non-believers and their doubts can range from mild to severe.

Note #2: The conversations in this book were polite, and while a few people may have become passionate or even rude, that was rare. Interreligious dialogue can and should be charitable and healthy even when two people disagree.

Note #3: At the end of each conversation, there may be different notes. These notes will offer practical advice on how to evangelize and share your faith more effectively.

Note #4: Some chapters may contain similar content to other chapters. The reason is for apologetics purposes. The more a person hears or reads something, the more they will retain that information in their head and be able to recall it when circumstances demand.

# CHAPTER 1

✙

# Why Is There So Much Pain?

### *Discussion with an Atheist about Suffering*

---

*Setting:* *A conversation with an atheist co-worker who was friendly, honest, and open-minded.*

Atheist: What do you do for a living?

Me: I am a Catholic speaker. I travel around and speak at retreats, conferences, and more. I speak to both adults and teens, and I love it!

Her: That's interesting. I don't really believe in God myself.

Me: Why not if you don't mind me asking?

Her: Mostly because there is too much suffering in the world. I have a hard time believing that a good and loving God would cause people to suffer.

Me: Do you think perhaps that you might be blaming God for the suffering of this world when He may have little or nothing to do with it?

Her: What do you mean?

Me: Let me give you an example. A man goes to a party and has far too much to drink. His friends attempt to shut him off, but he doesn't listen to them. Rather, he chooses to drink even more. When a friend tries to take his keys in order to prevent him from driving home, he almost gets in a fist fight with his own friend. Then, he proceeds to drive home drunk. On his way home, he hits and kills a child.

As horrific as this story is, one must ask: did God kill that child? Many people would blame God for this, but in reality, God had nothing to do with it. That man alone was responsible for his actions. He made one bad decision after another. It was he alone who chose to drink too much and to drive drunk even when his friends attempted to stop him.

Her: OK, I can see your point. That makes a bit of sense when you put it that way. [Thinking about it] But I have another question. Why would God allow that to happen? Why wouldn't He stop it?

Me: God *could* have stopped it. After all, He can do anything. However, He doesn't micromanage our lives or every choice that we make. He doesn't *force us* to change our minds or actions. Rather, He has given us an incredibly precious gift called free will. With this freedom, He asks us to do good and to make the world a better place. However, He gives us the freedom to make our own decisions. Obviously, some people choose poorly.

Her: [Butting in] Yes, but He *could* have stopped it.

Me: You're right, and since I'm not God, I don't know the reasons He chose not to. What I can tell you though is that if God is going to intervene and *force* people to do what's right in order to avoid all suffering, or if He is going to tinker with every outcome that's less than pleasant, then He has to take away our free will. God could have chosen to make us a race of robots that obey His every command. But, then we would not be capable of loving Him in return or having a relationship with Him – or with anyone else. Yet, it is a deep and intimate relationship that He desires to have with us.

He has given us free will and asks us to use it for good. Unfortunately, we know that some people abuse their free will and hurt others with it. With that being said, shouldn't we blame the people who make the bad decisions instead of God?

One more quick point: I personally know someone who was sexually abused, and she struggled with this for a long time in her relationship with God. This is a good example because she eventually came to God crying on her knees. The Lord healed her and made her new. Now she gives talks, shares her experience, and offers hope to others who have gone through the same trauma. If this had not happened to her, she wouldn't be able to minister to all the people she does.

13

Consequently, they would not receive the help or the hope they need.

So, while it was a horrible thing that happened, God brought so much good out of it, and continues to do so even to this very day. Additionally, this lady is far happier now than she has ever been before, even before the abuse, all because God changed her life for the better. Obviously, God never wanted this suffering in her life. However, He can transform any suffering into good if we allow Him.

Her: I'm still struggling with this, but I can see your point.

Me: Here is one last point to consider then. This is important for you to know. When God made the world, He made it perfect. It was mankind who brought pain and suffering into the world, not God. However, rather than leaving us to suffer alone in our misery, which we would have deserved, Christians believe that God made the choice to come to earth in the person of Jesus Christ all in order to enter into our suffering, to taste it, understand it, share it with us, and take it upon Himself.

Think about the person of Jesus for a moment. When Jesus walked on earth, He healed everybody who came to Him from things like: blindness, disease, sickness, sin, evil spirits, and every other painful illness.

Then, to take our sufferings for us and to redeem them, Jesus allowed Himself to be tortured and killed on the cross, one of the worst torture devices ever invented in the history of the world. However, when He rose in glory from the dead, He conquered and redeemed suffering in His body. In effect, *He reversed the curse* we caused from sin.

One reason Jesus performed countless healings and miracles was to show that *God never wanted suffering in the first place*. In addition, His conquering of sin and death was to be a foreshadowing of what He promises in heaven for those who follow Him. So remember, God is *not* the cause of suffering, but He *is* the cure for it! He can heal us if we run to Him with all of our hearts.

In heaven, no one will ever suffer again. The Bible teaches that the first thing God will do when we get to heaven is wipe away every tear from our eyes and remove all the pain from our hearts – for eternity! That is what we as Christians look forward to, and we invite everyone else to have this hope as well.

While God doesn't always intervene to stop tragedies and sorrows here on this earth, He can certainly help take away our own personal pain and suffering if we run to Him wholeheartedly. This is one thing I've personally learned in my own life. God healed me from many things and made me completely new.

Her: Thank you! I'll have to give this some more thought.

Me: Great! If you ever have any questions just let me know.

# CHAPTER 2

✛

# I Don't Believe In God

## *Conversation with an Atheist about God, Religion, and the Meaning of Life*

---

*Setting:* *This was a conversation with a lifeguard at the local swimming pool. One of the other lifeguards who I knew introduced us. We began by talking about novels but ended up in a discussion about God and life.*

Atheist: What do you do for a living?

Me: I'm a Catholic speaker and retreat leader. I speak to both adults and teens.

Her: Really? That's different. You won't like this, but I don't even believe in God.

Me: Why is that, if you don't mind me asking?

Her: Honestly, I'm not even sure. I have a lot of questions

about God and religion, and I am not really sure how to formulate them all.

Me: As already stated, I am a Catholic speaker who teaches the faith professionally and answers people's questions about God for a living. So, if you would like to ask me any questions at all, I would be more than happy to answer them for you. You'll find that I'm one of the nicest and easiest people to talk to on this subject. [I flash a really big smile.]

Her: Maybe I will then.

Me: Just so you know, I was always the person who asked deep questions but rarely received good answers. So, I feel it's important to have our questions answered. For me, it's like a puzzle. When you first begin a puzzle, it's just a chaotic pile of pieces. You may not even know where to start. However, as you begin to put some pieces in place, the picture begins to take form. As the picture starts to appear, it gets more exciting. When the puzzle is complete, you can see the whole picture and it all makes sense.

It's the same with God and religion. Many people don't have a strong belief in God because they have many questions, and it seems too chaotic to make any sense of it. This is completely understandable. However, for each question we get answered, it's like putting a new puzzle piece in place. You begin to see the picture starting to take shape and things begin to make more sense. Eventually, if we put enough pieces in place we can see the big picture. This usually leads us to a light bulb moment where we say,

"Aha, I get it! That makes complete sense!" And *that is* when religion becomes exciting, interesting, and begins to change your life!

Her: Like I said before, I'm not even sure where to begin or what questions I'd have. Like, we know nothing about God really. How do we even know God is there at all? It seems like we are just guessing. I mean, how do we know that aliens didn't create us or something? And, if there is a God, why does He allow so much suffering? I have a hard time seeing how God could be good and still allow suffering.

Me: Wow! Those are some *really* good questions, and very common ones that many people struggle with. So, where do we begin? What about with the question: "How do we know God exists, and how can we know who He is?"

Her: Yeah, that sounds good.

Me: OK great! Let's start with this. Imagine you are walking down the beach and you see a large heart drawn into the sand with the words, "Bryan loves Kathy" written inside. Then, you notice an arrow going through one side of the heart and coming out the other.

Now, would you ever think that the waves made that? That they pushed hard enough and in just the right way to make that heart? Or, would you say that an intelligent human being drew that heart in the sand?

Her: A person.

19

Me: Right. A different scenario: Imagine yourself walking through the hills of South Dakota and coming across four American presidents' faces carved out of the side of a mountain (Mount Rushmore). Would you naturally assume that those faces were just an accident, a random chance made by rain, wind, and erosion over a long period of time? Or, would you instinctively recognize that an intelligent person spent the greater part of their life carving those faces out of the side of the mountain?

Her: A person.

Me: Exactly! See, we are intelligent beings who *recognize other intelligence* when we see it. We identify that an intelligent person drew the heart and carved the faces. Just as we know that Mount Rushmore was created by an intelligent being and not by some accidental chance, so it's the same for the universe itself. We don't see creation as the product of accidental random chance (or trillions of random accidents) that all came about by nothing, from nothing, because of nothing, and for no reason whatsoever. Rather, it was designed by a higher intelligence and works toward a common end. Here's an example of what I mean.

We have the perfect amount of Oxygen, Hydrogen, Helium and other gases. If these were even the tiniest bit more or less, we wouldn't exist and neither would our universe. They are perfect for life. Also, we observe that the sun rises and sets every day, and the moon and stars light up the night after the sun goes down. We observe the universal constants, universal forces, gravity, and countless other things that all have their gauges perfectly set to the right dial, so to speak, in order for everything to exist.

Obtaining just one of these things (like gravity, for example) by accident is virtually impossible. Yet, there seem to be innumerable "impossibilities" that are somehow all possible and work perfectly together. We don't see this as just a random chance, but rather as the product of a higher intelligence that we call God. Just as it's clear that an artist created Mount Rushmore and used his chisel toward that end, so we observe rightly that a higher Intelligence made everything we know which also works toward a proper end.

But, how do we know it's God? Take a wristwatch and break it into the 100-120 individual working pieces that make it up. Next, place all of those pieces in a box; shake up the box vivaciously, and then dump the pieces out on the ground. Will you ever re-create the watch again doing it this way? Of course not. What you will find instead is a big mess.

Why? Because all of the pieces of the watch are *dead*. They cannot move, cannot self-assemble, cannot do anything because they are dead. If you leave them there long enough, they will disintegrate because *dead stuff does not do anything*!

Analogously speaking, it is the same with the universe. If there was only some dead stuff in the beginning which *somehow* popped into existence by itself; how did it move? How did it create? How did it make everything we know? It could not have because it is *dead*. Therefore, if there is anything in existence at all, there absolutely had to be an intelligent Higher Power who was *not* dead but alive, who *could* move, *could* create, and *could* bring about everything we know, and we call that being *God*. Does that make a little sense?

Her: Yeah, actually it does. It makes total sense.

Me: Another reason we believe God exists is because of Jesus. The real Jesus Christ of history (not the Jesus of Family Guy, the Simpsons, South Park, or other caricatures) reveals God and who He is. Anyone can come to the conclusion that there is a Creator of the universe, but who exactly is that Creator? How can we know Him? It is in and through the person of Jesus Christ that we can come to know God. Jesus came to bring us the fullness of truth and to reveal those things which we could never know.

Her: Yes, but haven't there been other great leaders from other religions? Don't those faiths believe *different* things about God? Don't their teachings contradict Jesus' teachings?

Me: Good question! [Excited] I love the fact that you are thinking deeply about this. Yes, there are other religions in the world, but I would argue that almost all of the major religions believe in the one same God. We are all in agreement there, though we may have different understandings of who He is. So, it all comes down to the person of Jesus Christ. For example, Moses and Abraham were *prophets* of God. Buddha preached *a way* to enlightenment. Muhammad claimed he was *a prophet*, a messenger of God, and so on.

All religious leaders have claimed to be *a* way to God or to higher enlightenment. However, Jesus Christ was totally different than everyone who came before and after Him. He claimed to be *the* very Son of God and claimed to have come directly from heaven. Moreover, He didn't just claim to be *a* way or *a* truth like all other religious leaders did. Rather, He claimed to be the *fullness of all truth* and *the only way* to heaven. That's a bold claim!

Now, either Jesus was telling the truth about that or lying. If His statements are true, then He is the greatest authority ever to walk the face of the earth. Consequently, we would need to believe in Him and follow Him. Why? Because we would know that what He teaches about God is true and can be trusted. However, if He was lying or mistaken, then we would need to go elsewhere and keep searching for truth.

That is why I say that it all comes down to the person of Jesus. If Jesus is right and He holds the full truth of God, then no other religious leader comes close to Him. They may preach some aspects of truth, but only Jesus would offer us the fullness of truth and the most perfect way to heaven.

Her: How do we know that Jesus is better than any of those other religious leaders? It seems to me that they were all good men, and that they all taught good things.

Me: Most of them were good men, but here's the difference.

Historically, we know that Jesus worked miracles, many miracles. He healed the blind with just a touch and the sick with just a word. He actually healed people who were deaf, paralyzed, and who had diseases. He raised people from the dead! What kind of power and authority must someone possess to be able to work miracles like that on command?

Not only did Jesus raise others from the dead, but He Himself rose from the dead. Jesus' miracles demonstrate His authority and verify that everything He claimed was true. Like a policeman showing you his badge to verify the fact that he's really a cop, so miracles authenticate the fact that Jesus had power and authority and can be trusted.

As nice as Buddha, Muhammad, Zoroaster, or any other religious leader might have been, they could not work miracles, could not forgive sins, did not claim ultimate authority, and did not rise from the dead. A simple overview of Jesus' life shows without a doubt that He is infinitely beyond any other religious leader.

Therefore, we can trust His words and can be assured that what He teaches about God and life are true. After all, that's why He came to earth in the first place: to show us the love of God, to reveal His truth, and teach us how to get to heaven.

Her: That makes a lot of sense. [Thinking deeply] But, how do we know, let's say, that aliens aren't real and didn't create the universe? Maybe *they* are the higher power?

Me: Well, that's not a bad theory. However, even if aliens are real, they could not be God or the creators of everything. Here is the reason why. About 13.7 billion years ago, an explosion occurred at a singularity, at a singular point that created everything including our universe. This is known as the Big Bang.

Science informs us that matter, energy, space, and time *came into existence* at *this point*. Since these things *came into* existence and had a *beginning*, they cannot be God, for God Himself is uncreated and eternal (without any beginning or end). Consequently, whatever created the universe *cannot* be made out of matter, like aliens for example, etc. Also the Creator cannot exist *within* space or time but transcends it.

Aliens are corporal beings, meaning that they are made out of matter, and therefore they themselves would have been created. Thus, aliens cannot be God or the creators of the material universes. Whatever or whoever is the Creator cannot be *part of the universe* but must transcend it in every way. Unlike aliens, the Creator cannot be made out of matter (but must be immaterial), nor can He be in time or space (meaning He must be timeless and spaceless, in short, eternal). Does that make sense?

Her: Yeah, it does.

Me: Great! Then, you must look at this evidence to see if you believe in God. You can look at the evidence regarding the universe and about the person of Jesus Christ to come closer to a conclusion.

Her: Hmmm. Well... I'd say that I probably believe in God then because all of that seems to make sense to me. But I guess... hmmm. [A new thought seems to enter her mind.] Even if God *does* exist, I don't see how or why I would need Him. I have a boyfriend who is great. My family and I are very close, and we have a deep love between us. Then, of course, my cats are always there for me too. I'm not trying to be mean or anything, and I kind of feel bad saying this, but I just don't think that I need God.

Me: That makes some sense from the perspective you are looking at it from. But, if you don't mind, I would like to help you see things from a different standpoint. It's like looking at a tree when you're standing right next to it versus looking at it from a mountaintop view surrounded by a thousand other trees. Obviously, it will be a completely different perspective from the top of a mountain.

So, let's zoom out and look at the whole picture with a different viewpoint. Let's begin by looking at the purpose of our life and why we are here in the first place. After all, we are all going to die someday. That's something all human beings have in common and have to consider. I don't mean to get all morbid, but even your cats are going to die someday and probably long before you. That's just nature.

Additionally, you may break up with your boyfriend in the future. Your parents too are getting older and will definitely pass away someday as well. So, it's possible that everything you currently love will not be there in the near future. Then what? What will you have left? Do you see my point?

Everything on this earth is temporary and fleeting. It's passing away. Imagine this: Imagine that the house next to us and this whole plot of land just disappears – all of the grass, trees, apartments, roads, etc. Gone. Now imagine that all of the buildings in the world disappear along with all of the people inside of them. Imagine in your mind the sky, space, stars, planets, gravity, and everything else vanishing forever. If you can, imagine complete and total nothingness. Stillness. Silence. Emptiness. *That* is the reality of the life we are living.

Even science confirms that our universe will cease to exist someday. In other words, all things are temporary. When everything is gone, you have a glimpse of what is really important. All that will be left is God and eternity. God is here among us right now, in fact. He permeates everything. He is eternal, unchanging, and not fleeting. When we die, there is eternity, heaven and hell, with God or without Him.

If we go to heaven, we will see family, friends, and all the other people we know and love who make it. We will be with them forever in a never-ending celebration. They will never die or be lost to us again.

The bottom line is this: we need to live with the end in mind. It cannot be just a nice idea or something we merely *hope* to attain. For this reason, we need God. We need that Someone who will always be there for us and who will never leave us. Our whole goal on this earth and the very reason we were made is to live with God, to love Him, and to be loved by Him for eternity.

You might not know it by looking at me, but I used to dress in all-black, carry weapons, and want to hurt people. I used to think about it, dream about it, and even wrote poetry about killing others violently. There was so much hatred and anger within me, and I was like a volcano always ready to explode, not to mention my constant depression, confusion, and rock-bottom self-esteem. I hardly looked in the mirror for seven years because I hated the person in the reflection. My whole life was one of self-hatred for a long time.

In any case, God came to me when I was at my worst. He changed my life and healed my heart. He took my hate and my rage and filled me to overflowing with great love. He took my confusion and gave me peace. He took my sadness, depression, and pain, and He filled me with a radiating joy and happiness! In short, God (Jesus) changed my life, fulfilled me, and gave me both meaning and purpose. That's the God I am speaking of, the God who is so good and Who is always there for us.

Her: Woah! I would have *never* known that about you! You seem so happy, friendly, and are so nice to talk to.

Me: [Big smile] Thank you!! What I'm saying here is that the God I'm speaking about is not an impersonal force or just a nice idea. He is a personal God, a relational God who wants a relationship with us. Just as you desire love from your boyfriend and family, He desires to love you and receive your love in return. As happy and complete as your life may seem now, I guarantee you that He can increase it 100 times over.

Her: Wow! That's kind of unbelievable everything that God did for you!

Me: Yes, it is. It's awesome!

Her: [She gets lost in thought. I decide to wait patiently and let her take as much time as she needed to think. After some silence, she seems to have another thought surface in her mind.] ... So, my mom is very religious. *Very* religious! She goes to Mass every day.

Me: [Jumping in] She does? Where?

Her: St. Mary's Church.

Me: No way! That's where I go. I have probably seen her and not even known it.

Her: How ironic. I'm going to tell her and see if she knows you. [Thinking deeply again] Sooo, my mother and some of my religious education teachers have talked a lot about sin and how angry God gets because of sin. Like, let's say I've said some bad words, or smoked, or killed someone, am I going to go to hell just because I did those things? Why would God even care if someone cursed anyway?

[*Interruption note:* At this point, I observed that the young lady was extremely open and had been eating up the truth about God. This openness is *rare*, a sign that God is working in her life. However, just because somebody can put belief in God doesn't necessarily mean that they are ready to commit their life to Him. Those are additional steps that they will need to grapple with. With her question here, it seems that this young lady was beginning to take steps down that path. It seems that she had received many false ideas about who God is which needed to be resolved if she was to ever come to know, accept, and follow Him.]

Me: Well, as I just said, God is a God of *love*. He changed my life and that's why I follow Him. It's not because I learned about Him in a book or went to Catholic school, but because He changed my life for the better. I also grew up believing that God was angry and was obsessed with punishing you over sin, but that was a misconception and not true. I now know that God loves me, and you too, and that He desires to change your life like you cannot even imagine.

In regard to sin, let's look at it this way. I mess up with my wife all the time, but she doesn't divorce me for merely getting impatient or losing my temper. Yet, some people believe God sends people to hell just for doing something small, that He flies off the handle over the tiniest sin. That is a completely false view of God and who He is.

Her: Yeah, but my mother presents God that way, as do other people.

Me: I know! I grew up hearing that line of thought too. Many people have presented God that way for sure, but that's not who He is, and you need to know that. *They* need to know that. God is perfect, right? So being perfect, would God be more or less loving than my wife?

Her: More.

Me: Yes, a lot more. Infinitely more! He is also infinitely more patient, kind, compassionate, and forgiving too. That makes sense, right? The more we understand this, the more we will understand that God is approachable. Regarding my own life, I have sinned thousands and thousands of times, and He still loves me. While God never approves of sin, He has never turned His back on me, and He has never walked away from me, not even once.

There are things I do wrong in my marriage, like losing my temper or being impatient, for example. However, when I apologize, my wife always forgives me. Through this, my wife and I actually grow even closer together. With that being said, what if I chose freely to abuse her, beat her, or cheat on her, for example. These would not be so easily forgiven. Things of this gravity have the possibility of separating us forever.

It's the same with God. Most sins we do are smaller in nature and do not break our relationship with Him. We apologize and try to do better. However, there are other sins that could break our relationship with God, things like murder, for example. It's not God who walks away at that point though, we do. Even then though, God would take us back if we repented and were truly sorry.

Religion isn't, or *shouldn't be*, about rules. Since I *love* my wife, I would never want to hurt her or do anything against her. It's the same with God. I follow Him out of love and because of His infinite and life-changing love for me. Just as I don't view the relationship with my wife as a set of rules, what I can and cannot do, so I don't view my relationship with God that way either, just a boring checklist of do's and don'ts. *It's all about love*! [Big smile]

Her: Well, I can see why we should not kill people or do big sins. That makes sense. I also like how you make God so loving and approachable. I like that. But, what about the smoking thing? If that's not really bad, could I do it?

Me: Hmmm. [I took a moment to ponder the best way to approach this question.] First, you need to know that God is not a micromanager. He gives you a certain amount of freedom to live your life and make your own choices. With that being said, God is omniscient and knows everything about us. He sees the future. He fully knows what is good for us and what will make us happy. Picture a parent who cautions a small child not to touch the hot stove. The child can't understand why, and yet, the parent can see the future, so to speak. They know with certainty that their child will be burned and so warn them to stay away.

It's the same with God. He knows us inside and out. He can see the future, and He cautions us to stay away from things that will burn us. That's sin. Sin burns us and hurts us, which is why God doesn't like it and warns us against it. However, in regard to other things like smoking, he's not going to necessarily make us stop, but He does love us so much that He desires for us to become the best people we can be. If that means that we stop smoking or cursing, so be it. Again, He won't make us, but being the good and loving Father that He is, He will always call us to do what is right. He will always encourage us to become better even when we cannot see what that is for ourselves. Does that make some sense?

Her: Yes! It does.

Me: [I react visually, surprised at how completely receptive this woman is and how God is working so strongly in her life.] Wow! I believe God has His hand on you and has a great plan for you. You are *very* open to all of these things which is a grace. A grace means that God is working in a special way in your life and that's *great*!! That's a *blessing*!

Her: Wow! That is an extremely nice thought. Hmm. [She begins to think silently again for a few moments.] Does this mean I have to go to church all the time and stuff? Because I don't see why I should have to go to church or follow a religion when I can just pray at home.

Me: Most people who *say* they can pray at home don't actually pray much or at all. That aside, you need to know that we are not just machines which obey orders that God programs us to obey. He is a personal being like we are Who desires a relationship with us. He *wants* a relationship with *you* just as you want one with your boyfriend. As a woman, I imagine that you want to be *desired* and *chosen* by another man. You want to be loved and so does God.

You don't have to become Mother Teresa and travel to India

to serve people who are poor and dying. I'm not even saying that you need to immediately go to church necessarily. Since you are just starting out here, you should at least begin by praying and talking to God. Ask Him to give you more faith and help you to see. Ask for understanding and for the ability to know His great love for you, and so on.

You have to remember that a relationship with God takes time. It's only baby steps sometimes but always moving forward. A relationship with Jesus is the most wonderful thing in the world. One thing you will discover about Jesus is that He is incredibly loving, fulfilling, and worth living for. He gives meaning to our lives. So, learn about Him more. Look into Him. Maybe open a Bible or pick up a good Catholic book on Jesus and read it. I mean, how did you fall in love with your boyfriend? You got to know him!

You talked *to* him, learned *about* him, and came to like him more and more. It's the same with God. In order to know Him, you have to learn about Him. Once you come to know God, you will see how infinitely lovable He is, and when you come to love Him and realize how much He loves you, then you will want to live for Him, serve Him, and give back to Him freely in return.

But it starts with baby steps. Start praying. Be honest and sincere with Him in how you feel. Also, I'd recommend picking up a Bible. Consider reading just one chapter a day every day, starting in the book of Matthew. Of course, you can skip the genealogy. Here you will learn all about Jesus and who He is, and you will see just how life-altering a relationship with Him can be. Obviously, He has changed my life for the better, and I know He wants to do the same for you! [Big smile]

[At this point, she became lost in thought again. I waited patiently not wanting to interrupt her thought process.]

*End Note:* This lady and I spoke for an hour, and it was a most pleasant and delightful conversation. I told her that anytime she had questions, it would be my pleasure to answer them. About a week later, I ran into her again and asked her if she had more questions. This turned into another one-hour conversation, after which, she put her faith in God and even made a commitment to start praying and going back to church. How awesome!

*Evangelization Note:* Religious discussions don't usually go this well. In just two conversations, this agnostic who wasn't even sure that God existed now understood with clarity what it takes many people years to comprehend.

She demonstrated with the utmost assurance that God's hand was on her and that His grace was working strongly in her life. She seemed blessed with the gift of understanding (one of the 7 Gifts of the Holy Spirit) and accepted everything with joy. I praised and thanked God all throughout the day for this and for using little me as His instrument. Naturally, I prayed for her too so God would continue to water the seeds He planted.

# CHAPTER 3

✠

# The Bible Is *Wrong*

## *Discussion on the Reliability of the Bible*

---

*Introductory Note:* Most Catholic teens are not shy to admit that they learned next to nothing in their years of religious education. So, when opportunity presents itself, I enjoy helping them to understand their faith in a way that makes sense and excites them.

*Setting:* One day, I decided to help quiz two girls for their upcoming Confirmation exam. A fervent atheist overheard us discussing religion and came to join our discussion.

Atheist:  What are you doing?

Girl # 1:  Learning information for our Confirmation test.

Him:  This guy is teaching you lies!

Me:  What?  Lies?  Why would you say that?

Him: I'm atheist, and I don't believe what you believe.

Me: You don't believe what I believe. That's fine, but do you actually think I'm intentionally lying to them?

Him: Well, I disagree with Christians and don't think there's any proof.

Me: Proof for what?

Him: For the Bible; I think that it's wrong. For example, archeologists can find no evidence at all for the Israelites being in Egypt. There's also no proof that a census ever happened with Jesus' family.

Me: So, you reject the whole Bible because archeology has thus far failed to provide these two historical occurrences? What about the thousands of discoveries archeologists *have* found that confirm the Bible again and again? By your very own reasoning then, you should believe in the Bible since there is far more evidence to support it.

Him: Maybe, but there is still absolutely no evidence of the Israelites being in Egypt.

Me: If that's true, I would say there isn't any evidence *yet.* However, there are many other things archeologists have claimed the Bible was wrong about and then had to reverse their positions when new discoveries were made.

For example, archeologists could not find any evidence for

Pontius Pilate whatsoever. They concluded that the Bible was mistaken in that regard. Then, lo and behold, they found unmistakable evidence for Pontius Pilate. The same thing happened with the two cities of Sodom and Gomorrah. Archeologists thought that Sodom and Gomorrah were a myth until they excavated those cities some years ago.

Also in the Bible, Luke mentions Lysanias the Tetrarch who was a ruler. The problem for Archeologists was that they could only find a Lysanius 50 years later and in another region. Naturally, they concluded that the Bible was mistaken. However, two inscriptions for Lysanias the Tetrarch have been discovered in recent times exactly at the time and place St. Luke had stated.[3]

In addition, Herod the Great was also considered to be a myth, so said archeologists. But again, in very recent times, they excavated large amounts of Herod's palace in Israel to prove the Bible right yet again. The evidence is clear, and I could give *many* more examples, but I think you get the point. Just because there is no evidence now for something now doesn't mean there won't be in the future.

Him: Alright, good points. [The atheist just turns and walks away.]

*End Note:* There were three girls listening to the whole conversation and grinning from ear to ear. They were happy that someone finally stood up to that atheist. My hope was

---

[3] *The Case for Christ*, by Lee Strobel (Chapter 4).

that everyone present saw that it is reasonable to believe in the Bible and that the Catholic religion doesn't just have blind faith but provides good and logical reasons for her beliefs.

# CHAPTER 4

✠

# What About Aliens?

## *And Other Brief Conversations*

---

*Introduction Note:* Sometimes all a person needs is a key question or two in order to help them see the error of their thinking or to reconsider their position. This was the case in some of the following discussions. The art of asking good questions is a gem in the field of evangelization.

*Setting:* A polite conversation with a co-worker. When he found out that I was a Christian, he immediately let me know where he stood on the question of God.

Him: I don't believe in God.

Me: [Politely] Really? Why Not?

Him: Because I don't believe in things I can't see.

Me: Hmmm.  Can I ask you a question?

Him: Sure.

Me: Do you believe in aliens?

Him: Yes.

Me: Why?

Him:  Because the universe is so infinitely vast.  There *has* to be something else out there besides us.

Me: Have you seen any aliens?

Him:  No but chances are well in our favor that there is something else out there.

Me:  I thought you said you don't believe in things that you can't see?

Him:  [Realizing the contradiction] Touché. Good point.

~      ~      ~

*Setting:  After giving a 45-minute presentation on evidence for the existence of God, I noticed a sad looking high school girl after the talk.  She was dressed all in black and looked like death.  When the lunch break arrived, I decided to strike up a conversation with her. The short conversation was put in this book to demonstrate the point that many people reject God without good reasons for doing so, or in some cases, without any reason at all. This is called emotional atheism. Everyone, both theists and atheists, needs to study the question of God and not just blindly make a decision. It's the most important question in our life!*

Me: Hey! How do you like the retreat so far? [Big smile]

Her: I hate it.

Me: *Hate* it? How come?

Her: I'm an atheist. I don't believe in God.

Me: Interesting. So, I'm curious. Why are you an atheist, and why don't you believe in God?

Her: I don't believe in anything.

Me: I know that, but *why*?

Her: Because I don't.

Me: Yes, you just said that. But you have to have reasons for not believing in God. What are those reasons?

Her: I just don't think there is any evidence.

Me: No evidence? What about all of the evidence I just presented for the last 45 minutes? What did you think about everything I said?

Her: I just think all you Christians are brainwashed. No offense, but I think you are all stupid for believing what you do.

Me: [Surprised] Stupid? [Very nicely] So, you think that our beliefs are stupid even though I just gave 45 minutes of logical and deductive proofs, and you cannot even give me one good reason for being an atheist.

Her: Well, I still don't believe.

Me: Hmmm. Well, I will certainly pray for you. [I give her a sincere and loving smile.]

*Apologetics and Evangelization Note:* It's important to always listen to the Holy Spirit when evangelizing. For example, in this conversation, I could have held this girl's feet to the fire using her own contradictory logic against her. However, listening to the Spirit, I felt that there were deeper emotional issues present. As stated above, this is a clear case of "emotional atheism."

Emotional atheism is when someone rejects God and religion but cannot give any good reasons why. This is because the reasons are more emotional than intellectual. Therefore, they must be dealt with in an entirely different way. Emotional atheists and agnostics have often experienced some sort of suffering, pain, or abuse in life, although the problem could be laziness, sloth, or rebellion too. (These last three are more common in agnostics rather than atheists).

Perhaps they were physically, emotionally, or even sexually abused growing up or lost a loved one. Believing that God is powerful and loving, they cannot grasp how or why God would let these bad things happen. Some struggle at first and then slowly drift away not being able to make sense of it all. Others lose their faith cold turkey. Their "disbelief" is more of an anger toward God or the result of feeling abandoned by Him. This is understandable.

Since I felt that was the case here, I chose not to push the issue. You cannot use rational thought with people who only think emotionally! You have to find another way around their walls. Love and unconditional acceptance work well. The evangelist may possess all the right answers, but if the other person is not open or just refuses to hear it, there's not much you can do except plant a few seeds and move on. Just make sure that you water those seeds with much prayer after the conversation. The more you pray, the more the seeds will be watered by God.

~     ~     ~

*Setting*: *This was taken from an actual conversation of an atheist attacking me on social media.*

Atheist: God is not real!!

Me: You sound so sure. Can you prove that, and can you give me evidence to back up your statement?

Him: You cannot prove a negative, but you *can* prove a positive. So go ahead, prove that God is real!

Me: Nice try, but that is a copout answer. You were the one who first stated "God is not real," so it is *you* who need to offer some evidence to support your claim, unless of course, your nonbelief is based on nothing at all.

Him: Explain pediatric cancer, and if you say God is testing us, then why does he allow animal abuse? Catholics believe animals don't have souls, so why does he need to test them? If God is real, then He is a sociopathic power abusing monster, and I fail to see a reason to worship that.

Me: First, Catholics believe animals have souls. They are just different than human souls. Second, your original statement was that "God is not *real*," not *God is not nice* or worthy of worship. You mentioned that people and animals suffer, but that doesn't do anything to disprove God.

At most, it demonstrates that He's not "good" or that He allows suffering for a greater purpose. Perhaps *we* are the ones who create most of the diseases and sufferings in this world. In other words, there are a whole host of possible answers that could be debated, but they don't disprove God. So, try again.

Him: As I previously stated, you cannot prove a negative, but proving a positive is not only possible, it's easy. So, prove to me that God exists.

Me: It doesn't seem like you can back up your original statement or give evidence to show that God is not real. I realize you cannot *disprove* God's existence, but you *can* offer evidence to back up your statement and show that it is reasonable. If you have no evidence, perhaps you should not make such a bold claim.

Him: The burden of proof is on you.

Me: Actually, the burden of proof is on *both sides*. Each side makes a claim and therefore must be able to provide evidence to back up that claim. Since you made the first remark, the burden of proof is on you.

Him: How about this then. God is not observable in any manner whatsoever. Now give me evidence He *does* exist!

Me: Hold on a second. You said God isn't observable, but that doesn't demonstrate He is not real. Just because you yourself haven't seen God and aren't acquainted with the evidence, that doesn't mean He's not real.

At one time, there were whole universes that were not observable, but over time, we have discovered them. These were real and *in existence* long before we had the capability of discovering them. There are millions of things in space we don't have the capability to see, observe, or detect right now, but that doesn't mean they are not real but only that we are limited beings. Moreover, God is observable in different ways. So again, just because you haven't personally experienced Him doesn't mean He's not real. After all, you have never seen the Holocaust, gravity, or aliens, and yet probably believe they exist.

Him: Well, your church hates gays. Who are they to claim two people that love each other cannot get married? What gives them the right to play moral cop in the world? The church is outdated and needs to get up with the times.

Atheist #2: [Another atheist enters the online conversation at this point.] Excuse me. I'm an atheist too, but I don't believe in harassing theists, especially good theists like Bryan. He is a good guy, so leave him alone.

*End Note*: The conversation ended there. The bottom line is that this atheist could not disprove God or offer good evidence for his disbelief. In addition, his last statement revealed the *real* issue he had with religion. As with many people who *choose* not to believe in God, it's not because of a lack of evidence. Rather, it is often for moral reasons or because they do not wish to follow certain rules.

~     ~     ~

<u>*Setting*</u>: *I ran into my neighbor outside, and we just shot the breeze for a few minutes before this conversation happened.*

# What About Aliens?

Him: What do you have going on tonight?

Me: I am teaching Bible study.

Him: Really? Good for you. I'm not into that myself, but that's a good thing to be interested in. At least you're not like those Catholics who contradict the Bible. [This came out of nowhere. This man never even asked if I was Catholic but just made assumptions.]

Me: I didn't know that the Catholic Church contradicted the Bible. Could you give me some examples of these contradictions?

Him: [Caught off guard] Umm... well... actually... I can't think of any right now, but you know those Catholics, right?

Me: [Dryly] Ah, those Catholics. Surely, you must be able to think of some contradictions though.

Him: Umm, I can't really think of any right now.

Me: Uh huh. Well, you let me know when you do, and we can talk about it.

~    ~    ~

*Setting: A conversation with a bitter, anti-religious co-worker in the lunch room. This particular conversation demonstrates that people often cling to their beliefs whether they are rational or not.*

Bitter Teacher: [Speaking generally to the teachers at the lunch table] My son tells me that he doesn't believe in God, and when we went to church recently for a funeral, he didn't want to receive communion because he had not gone to confession first. I asked him why he would go to confession if he didn't believe in God.

Teacher #2: [Interrupting] Wait, people still believe in Confession? Does anyone even do that anymore?

Me: [Enthusiastically] I do!

Teacher #2: You do? *Really?*

Me: Oh yeah! All the time; I know many other people who do too.

Bitter Teacher: Well, why would a supposedly loving God send someone to hell?

Me: You are a *teacher* and you are asking that question? That's like a parent asking why her son who did absolutely nothing all year received an F in your class. It can also be likened to a student who says, "Mr. Smith is nice, he would not give me an F. I didn't do an ounce of work all year, but he will pass me."

You know as well as I do that teachers don't give students

an F. Each student earns their own grade by what he or she does and does not do. As a teacher, you merely give them the grade they deserve. Now if they plead with you, you may have mercy and allow them extra credit or something, but in the end, they still receive the grade they earn.

Him: [Dismissing and ignoring an explanation that was perfectly logical] Yeah, but why would a loving God send someone to hell?

Me: Why would you give someone an A who deserves an F? If he received zeros on everything, would you not fail him? [I was going to explain more, but teacher #2 jumped in again.]

Teacher #2: You are not going to win this one. Bryan is very religious and goes to church a lot.

Him: That's fine. If he wants to go to church, that's his problem.

*End Note 1:* I left the conversation there, resisting the urge to respond with a whirlwind of evidence about the topic in order to help him understand it more or about his own justifications. As a teacher, he should have been able to understand the comparison I was making, but he did not want to for there were many deeper issues there, which is why I chose to drop it.

Another comparison can be likened to a boyfriend who hardly ever speaks to his girlfriend even though he's dating her. He's sad and miserable around her and doesn't do anything to try to make her happy. He doesn't think about her when they are apart and doesn't miss her when she's away on vacation. Worse, he comes to life and becomes instantly happy when he hangs out with other pretty girls. He talks to them with joy and even flirts with them.

His girlfriend observes how he interacts with *other* girls and complains to him often about it. The boyfriend blurts out, "What's the problem? I'm a good person. I do good things for people. That must count for something." The girlfriend will respond, "A good person? Well, not to me you're not."

This is like our relationship with God. We do not create good relationships with our family, friends, or anyone else merely by wishing for them and then doing nothing. We have to want a relationship with someone and then work hard to deepen it and make it great!

Likewise, we will not get to heaven or have a relationship with God by accident or by doing nothing (by just claiming to be a good person). That won't do anything for us. We need to cultivate and foster a deep relationship with God as we would with someone on this earth who we love.

*End Note 2:* Again, here we have an example of emotional atheism. This teacher did not reject God for rational reasons but for emotional ones. I made the decision to just pray for him. If only this teacher knew that God is not a kill-joy but the *source of all joy*! If only this man knew that God wants to fulfill his every desire more than he could ever imagine!

## What About Aliens?

Many people have grown up with the idea that God is angry, emotionally distant, and far removed from our problems. Who would want a relationship with someone like that? However, this picture of God is false, and people will never come to know God deeply with false understandings of who He is.

That is why it's crucial that we not only present who God is, but authentically model His joy and love in both our words and actions. If people do not see it in you, they may never see it at all!

# CHAPTER 5

✠

# There Is No Proof For God

## *A Conversation with a Militant Atheist*

---

*Setting: While substitute teaching a high school science class, an atheist noticed that I was reading a book about science and the Catholic Church.*

Militant Atheist: Hey, I see that you're reading a book about science. What book is it?

Me: Yes! The book is called, "The Catholic Church and Science: Answering Questions and Exposing the Myths."

Him: That sounds interesting, what is it about?

Me: It seeks to answer the myths which claim that the Catholic Church is against science. In fact, it shows how the Catholic Church loves science and has always worked hard to advance its cause.

Him: [Intrigued] Really...

Me: Yes! Contrary to many myths floating around, the Church has never been against science. She accepts the Big Bang theory and doesn't necessarily see evolution as a problem or a contradiction when properly understood.

Him: [The atheist jumps in cutting me off] But evolution *does* contradict the Bible and the Catholic religion. You believe in a creation of seven literal days while scientists know that creation happened over billions of years. Also, where does the Bible even mention dinosaurs?

Me: The Bible says that God created *all* things, the beasts of the earth and birds of the air. This would include dinosaurs and other creatures not mentioned in the Bible. You must remember that the Bible is not a science book or an encyclopedia. It's a *spiritual* book written to communicate spiritual lessons primarily.

Additionally, many people seek to interpret the Bible from an *American* point of view and with a *modern* day understanding. In Biblical interpretation, it's essential to recognize what the original author himself was trying to communicate. In this case, the author of Genesis wasn't trying to tell us *how* everything happened nor was he attempting to give a scientific explanation of creation.

The point he was trying to make was that God created all things. It might also be helpful for you to know that the Catholic Church does not teach creationism, the notion that the earth was made in seven literal days. After all, the sun, moon, stars and other heavenly bodies used to tell time were not even created until the fourth day, meaning that they could not be literal 24 hour days. It's the same with Adam and Eve. The Bible says that Adam and Eve were the first two created people. Scientifically speaking, it could just mean that they were the first two homo sapiens.

If God desired to bring about life by way of evolution, where is the contradiction? I'm sure you have read in the news recently that scientists and archeologists said the whole human race can be traced back to one man and one woman. Everyone comes from these two people. So, that seems to confirm this too, no?

Him: [Reluctantly] Yeah, that makes some sense, I guess. But why even believe in a God in the first place? There is no proof for God.

Me: I take it you don't believe?

Him: Nope. I'm an atheist! I already didn't believe in God, but then I read *The God Delusion* by Richard Dawkins, and he just blows religious belief out of the water.

Me: No, he doesn't, not at all. I've read his book, and it doesn't disprove anything. In fact, there is a lot of good evidence for the existence of God that he fails to mention.

Him: Like what?

Me: Like the fact that *something can't come from nothing.* Imagine nothing for a moment. No trees, oxygen, or gravity. They don't exist. No stars, space, energy, sky, anything. If you imagine black space or empty space in your mind, that's still *something.* Imagine pure nothingness if you can. It's extremely hard to do.

If there was absolutely nothing at one time, then there would still be nothing now because something can't come from nothing. We would not be here – nothing would. After all, things that don't exist... *don't exist!* If there was only absolute nothingness, then something could not have appeared because *there wasn't anything to come into existence* in the first place.

Let me give you an example from Fr. Robert Spitzer that he uses.[4] He says that the number 0 symbolizes nothing. If you take zero and add a thousand more zeros, it still equals zero. If you add a million zeros or even a trillion, trillion, trillion, trillion zeros, you still get 0. So, to sum it up: $0 + 0 = 0$ and $0 + 00000000000000000000000000000 = 0$. It is always zero and can never be anything else. It's the same with nothing. Nothing + Nothing = Nothing. Always and forever. You can't get something from nothing. Therefore, there *had* to be Someone who existed by His very nature already who could bring everything else into existence.

Him: That's a good point, except that in the quantum field

---

[4] This example comes from Fr. Spitzer's book, *New Proofs for the Existence of God.*

science tells us that things come into and go out of existence from nothing all the time.

Me: Actually, they originate inside of a quantum vacuum which you know is a sea of fluctuating energy. Energy is not nothing but something. A vacuum is also not nothing but something. As I have already stated, if there was absolutely *nothing*, there would not even be a quantum vacuum, energy, or anything else. Period. *From nothing comes nothing.* Forever. Therefore, for anything to exist at all, there *had* to be an eternal Being who possessed existence by His very nature. We give that being the name *God.*

Him: Why does it have to be God?

Me: What else would it be? Who else is a being of pure existence powerful enough to create universes and bring something into existence from nothing?

Him: It's possible that we could have come from other universes. There are other theories such as string theory, a bouncing universe, or even a multi-verse where our universe would just be one of countless others going back forever.

Me: So basically, what I'm hearing is that you would accept that the universe can be eternal but not God – that an infinite amount of potential and contingent[5] universes are the cause of all the universes and have no cause themselves? This is

---

[5] The argument for God's existence from contingency and efficient causality will be discussed in chapter 12.

amazingly unscientific. You who love science propose an unscientific theory that could never be proven. It seems to me that you are willing to believe in things that have no creative power but won't believe in a Being with actual creative power. [I'm interrupted at this point by another student who jumps in.]

Girl #1: [Annoyed at the stubbornness of the atheist] Sometimes, you just have to believe. Sometimes, there is no proof. You just need to have faith.

Him: [This sends the atheist into a fit of anger. He starts yelling at the girl.] See, that's *exactly* what I *hate*! I *hate* people who have no answers, who just blindly believe in a fairy in the sky!

Me: [To the girl] Please don't claim that there is no proof just because you yourself haven't studied it. There *is* evidence. What do you think I've been trying to give all this time? [Speaking super kindly to the atheist] Let's get back to our discussion.

Girl #2: You guys aren't even allowed to talk about religion in school.

Him: [Getting fiery again, he whirls around and snaps at this girl too.] Actually, we *are* allowed to talk about it. I'm just asking him questions, and he is allowed to answer my questions. If you don't know the law and don't know what you are talking about, please don't talk!

Me: [My eyebrows perk up in surprise.] Wow! I'm impressed that someone actually knows the law. Good job! [I give him a little mock applause.]

Him: [Talking to the two girls] Just because you don't know anything, don't blame Mr. Mercier. At least he has thought about this and is giving some good answers. [He turns back to me more calm and rational.][6] Mr. Mercier, you have to admit though that you really don't know God exists.

Me: What about the evidence I just gave you?

Him: But we don't know *anything* yet. It could be anything. Science has taught us so much disproving a lot of what religion held to be true, but we still don't know anything. We can't see most of the known universes and certainly not beyond them. We may discover other things someday which disprove God. Basically, it comes down to this: science will teach us everything we need to know. If it can't be proven by science, how could we ever believe it? Science is the only study and practice that gives us facts. Religion cannot do that.

Me: Science could never tell us *everything* we need to know as demonstrated by the fact that you could never prove that statement scientifically. If you go solely by science, then

---

[6] While this atheist got passionate at times, he never yelled or got angry with me, only at people who chimed in with comments that were not well thought out. We ourselves had a great conversation.

you need to show me right now with conclusive scientific proof that science will absolutely prove every last thing. Show me the evidence of that as a fact and *not* just in theory or as something that might seem probable. What you're suggesting is a colossal assumption.

Him: Science has proven so much already though. It's just a matter of time before we find out other answers.

Me: Again, that's a huge assumption, not a fact, and certainly not something you can prove scientifically. Otherwise, you would be able to show me the facts to prove it right now. Just because science has proven many things doesn't naturally lead to the conclusion that it will be able to prove everything or even has the ability to – especially the supernatural.

You don't even know if science has the ability to detect the divine or if it ever could. Show me the experiments done that prove or disprove God. The fact is, we don't even know what's outside our limited amount of universes that we can see, as you yourself said. If we can't see or detect over 90% of *material things* that exist, how could we ever sanely consider that we can scientifically detect divine and supernatural things using means like science?

That doesn't even make sense because by definition science deals only with natural things that can be observed and tested through repeated experiment. God cannot be seen, observed, or tested by any natural means. He can't be put under a microscope. We can't concoct some experiment that says,

"See, there's God." Therefore, science cannot have any say in the matter of religion. The best you can do is to say that it's *more reasonable* to believe that God does or does not exist for the reasons of x, y, and z.

Him: The burden of proof is on you.

Me: Actually, it's not. Both sides, atheists and theists, are making claims. Therefore, both sides need to present evidence. You have no evidence that God does not exist. If you do, present it, and I'll present mine, and we can discuss it. Or, at least, show me why you believe it's more reasonable that God does *not* exist.

Him: There's also no proof that the Flying Spaghetti Monster exists or a tiny tea pot in space. They could. There's no proof either way just like your God.

Me: The *big* difference is that *nobody* actually believes in a Flying Spaghetti Monster (FSM) whereas most of the entire world believes in God or an all-powerful creator Being. The Big Bang demonstrates that all matter, energy, space, and time *came into existence* at the moment of the Big Bang. So, if matter came into existence and the FSM is made out of matter, then that means even if he does exist, he is not eternal, and therefore cannot be God.

But, there's no proof for the FSM whereas there is much proof for God. Jesus Christ is just one of the many proofs for God. He claimed to come from God and backed Himself up with countless miracles on command. He healed people who were blind, deaf, paralyzed, and rose people from the dead. Miracles still happen today in His name.

Then, there is demonic possession, people being raised from the dead, and much more all happening today – many scientifically verified. Moreover, since the FSM is made out of spaghetti, it would decompose in no time at all and cease to exist. So, Christians can present evidence for God, whereas the FSM has no good evidence whatsoever. Therefore, the FSM is not plausible or even reasonable. To this point, it's just a made up parody "religion" which is evidence against it too.

Him: Well, you mentioned miracles. I do not believe in miracles. [In an exaggerated mocking tone] "Oh, my arm hurts from a soccer game, but then I prayed and now it feels better." That's not miraculous! Heck, we don't even know that Jesus really existed!

Me: How could you not believe Jesus existed? Everyone believes that. It's a historical fact. Only people on the extreme fringe don't accept this fact.

Him: Is there *any* proof for Jesus outside of the Bible? Any whatsoever?

Me: Absolutely! Virtually every encyclopedia, history book, and historian in existence are all in agreement that Jesus existed. But if you are talking about source material from the time of the Bible, that is available too. There were Roman *and* Jewish historians in the first century who wrote about

Jesus and confirm Biblical details. Josephus, for example, was a Jewish historian who wrote about Jesus, and Tacitus was a Roman historian who did too. Pliny the Younger was an author, a lawyer, and a magistrate in the Roman Empire who also mentions Jesus. Even the Jewish Talmud talks about the existence of Jesus, His disciples, and how the disciples worked miracles in His name, etc.

Him: Well OK, fine. But, even *if* there was evidence for Jesus, that's a far cry from being able to work miracles. His disciples probably just made that up. Miracles don't happen. They can't happen!

Me: Yes, they certainly do happen even today.

Him: [Getting passionate] No, they don't! It's impossible for miracles to occur. There is a natural explanation for everything. People just make up miracles because they need to believe in some superior force for which they have no proof.

Me: Actually, there is a lot of proof. And, how do you know for certain that miracles cannot happen and are not possible, even in rare circumstances? You are coming to the table with pre-formed conclusions and without looking at the evidence. That is not very scientific you know.

Him: I know the evidence! People claim that everything is a miracle. [In a mocking tone again] "My Grandmother did not die in a car crash, it's a miracle." Or, "I fell off my bike and nothing happened, it's a miracle."

Me: Yes, that's partly true. Some people do throw the word miracle around, but those aren't true miracles or the proper definitions of one. They're just nice sayings. A real miracle is the suspension of the laws of nature. Take for example; a blind person being prayed over who suddenly receives his sight back at the name of Jesus. This is far more miraculous; wouldn't you agree? Or, take a person who has an incurable disease which immediately vanishes when they are prayed over in the name of Jesus. These are miraculous in nature.

Him: These things don't actually happen though.

Me: They totally do! You just choose not to believe them.

Him: Even if they did, there could be natural explanations for them, and those are far more likely.

Me: Certainly. It is possible there could be some natural explanation, and the Catholic Church is open to that, but...

Him: So why do you believe that miracles are definitely God then?

Me: There are other proofs for God I haven't mentioned yet that prove his existence much more solidly. Miracles are a bit different though. So, I'm not saying the evidence of miracles is 100% conclusive like 2+2=4. What I'm saying is that God seems to be the best explanation of these occurrences. You don't have mass amounts of atheists being healed from some of the most incurable diseases known to mankind. Yet, isn't it odd that people are continually healed in the name of Jesus when Christians pray over them. People are even healed from things like tuberculosis or from being paralyzed. Those aren't small.

Girl #3: There's obviously a God, so you should just believe.

Him: [He instantly flashes to anger – his face almost red.] You want me to believe blindly like all you other lemmings? [To the girl] OK, go ahead! Give me some proof that God exists.

Me: [Speaking very calmly to him so as to bring him back to a rational discussion] Can we just ignore that and get back to what we were discussing?

Him: OK. Here's my problem. I go by science. Science is fact. If science can't prove miracles or demonstrate their reality, then I'm not going to believe them.

Me: You'll probably be surprised to learn that science *has* verified many miraculous occurrences even after extensive and rigorous testing. There are many examples, but here is just one: the miracle of the two atomic bombs in Japan.

During World War II, two atomic bombs were dropped on two different cities in Japan – Hiroshima and Nagasaki. An atomic bomb, as you may know, is well over 30,000 degrees (Fahrenheit) incinerating and disintegrating everything in its path. Yet, at both Hiroshima and Nagasaki, two houses belonging to Catholic priests still stand today. Both houses were in very close proximity to the blast (about 8 blocks away, I think). Yet, their houses are still intact, and the priests are still alive without any major harm done to them.

Every other house and building in all directions were completely leveled in less than a second. Even people 100 times the distance of the bomb died from radiation, and yet, the Catholic priests at both locations were completely and amazingly untouched by radiation and their houses intact.

Him: I don't believe that for a second.

Me: Come on, you're smart! Do some research. Look it up for yourself. If you don't believe, it's because you're disbelieving blindly, which is ironically what you accuse religious believers of doing.

The fact is that a team of *200 scientists* did experiments and tests on these priests for years and found absolutely nothing wrong with them. Scientists have documented this, and since you said you believe things that science confirms, you should be more than inclined to believe this. [At this point, the atheist goes completely quiet and begins to think deeply about it all. I give him some time and then continue. Thinking back, I probably should have given him more time until *he* broke the silence. Live and learn.]

That is just one example. You could also investigate the miracles at Lourdes, in France. There have been thousands and thousands of people healed from many different ailments including some of the most incurable diseases known to mankind.

Him: [Suddenly agitated a bit] No, no, no, no...

Me: Hold on, can I finish please?

Him: Sure, sorry.

Me: It's well documented that two women came to visit Lourdes on the same day. They were both blind. One of the blind women was born with no pupils in her eyes. Ironically, they were *both* healed. Here's the odd thing: the woman who had no pupils still did not have any even after she was healed. Yet, she could see perfectly. That really happened, and that's just one example of many.

In fact, since you love science, you should know that sixty-seven of these miracles at Lourdes have been *scientifically verified*, meaning they have been studied and substantiated by scientists, some of whom were not even Christian. So, science does help verify the authenticity of some miracles.

Him: I don't believe that. You have no proof. Did she even see a doctor?

Me: What do you think? Of course she saw a doctor! Her doctor was flabbergasted and had no words, no explanation of how she could see. Yet, she can.

Him: I don't believe that. Her doctor could be in on the whole thing.

Me: Oh, come on now! Be honest. Even if he was somehow

in on it, Lourdes has a whole panel of doctors and physicians who check these people out. It's not like some religions that just *claim* miracles happen but without any witnesses. In the Catholic faith, the Church does not hesitate to bring other people in to have the phenomena verified (or rejected). Again, some of these people are not even believers and therefore have no bias.

Him: They could all be in on it, how do we know?

Me: OK! I'm the one here giving *actual evidence*, and all you're doing is deflecting the evidence with baseless conspiracy theories and blind skepticism. You made it clear that you liked science and that you "only go by science." Yet, you won't even believe science when it's inconvenient for you to do so. That's dishonest. So, tell me, what kind of a miracle would you need to see in order to believe it's miraculous?

Him: Hmmm. Probably someone who has one leg shorter than the other and is healed instantly – someone's bone growing out or something like that.

Me: That would be miraculous, and it's happened many times.

Him: [Shaking his head] Don't believe it!

Me: Of course you don't. You haven't even looked at the evidence either way in order to refute it. Moreover, you refuse to study the evidence. Listen, no one can make you believe these miracles, but they happen nonetheless. And it's not like they happened over 2000 years ago in Biblical times. Many of these miracles are modern day. Other people have witnessed the miraculous occurrences. In addition, they are checked out at length by doctors and physicians.

Their family and friends know them before the miracle and after. Thus, the evidence is clear. You say you love science but you don't believe science when it's inconvenient. Many miracles have been scientifically verified, and so if you truly loved science, you would listen to what they say and believe.

Him: [In a snappy tone] Why doesn't God heal everyone then if He is real? Why does He play favorites?

Me: I do not know the reason why God chooses to heal some people and not others, but there are a few possible explanations. First, God is not Santa Clause who merely brings us everything we want. He is also not an almighty vending machine who dispenses our every request. Rather, God gives us what we need when we need it, and what's best for us. Only He knows what that is.

As humans, we cannot know what will take place 30 seconds or even 10 seconds from now, and yet, God can see every future occurrence with perfect clarity. Therefore, He knows our needs. He knows the outcome of all decisions and events. He fully comprehends what is good for us and what is not, what will lead us to Him and what will lead us away from Him. Perhaps, God knows that if a person is granted their request, it will destroy them over time.

Second, Jesus Himself taught that a person must have great faith in order to see great works. Perhaps some people have a strong faith while others do not. Also, it might not be the appropriate time. I know people who have been healed right away while others have been healed at a later time. A third reason God may allow suffering is to remind us of our dependence on Him. People who get too comfortable in life see no need for God and often turn away from Him.

*End Note:* At this point, the bell rang telling us that class was over. This hardened atheist was thinking deeply about everything we discussed. He told me that he *thoroughly enjoyed* our discussion, and that he loved conversing with someone who "actually knew what he was talking about." Truth be told, I enjoyed the conversation too.

*Apologetics Note:* I think that most people who read this conversation would see that there is very good evidence for God. Some people are stubborn because they truly don't understand and they want to test the strength of the opposing arguments.

However, more often than not, angry and stubborn people have some emotional obstacles that they need to overcome, or they don't wish to change their lives, or there is some other hidden reason like this. This is even more evident when they become irrational and stop arguing soundly. You can bet that there is something else going on, something else not being said, a deeper issue.

Some people have a personal gripe with God or the Church.

Some are angry with God over some perceived slight. I have found that the people who are most angry and adamantly opposed to God/Christianity have had something bad happen in their life. They have experienced a huge tragedy or some great suffering.

Or many times, there is sin or addiction in their life that is incompatible with living for God that they perhaps don't recognize or wish to acknowledge. Sometimes, the most convenient way to deal with this is just "not to believe." Their pick with God is an emotional one based on brokenness or sin and is usually projected into doubt, anger, or severe skepticism, no matter what the evidence is.

This is important to know because these hardcore skeptics will bombard you with many reasons for why they don't believe and for why God doesn't exist. However, these are usually smokescreens and are almost never the real issues. The bigger reasons for unbelief are much deeper and must be mined for. Our job is to listen not only with our ears to their objections, but with our hearts to the deeper issues that may be present.

For example, the late Christopher Hitchens was known as one of the biggest religion haters on the planet. His goal was to destroy people's faith, to sow doubt and confusion, and to make everyone an atheist. He was angry, hostile, and often brewed internally. After Christopher's death, his brother Peter (who was also an atheist but converted to Christianity) revealed the whole story.

He divulged the fact that in their early childhood, their mother ran away with a Protestant pastor. Then, in a hotel room, the two of them committed suicide together. The little Hitchens boys never saw their mother again. If this horrific situation had happened to me, I would probably hate religion with all my heart too.

The point is that the more anger someone has toward God or religion, the more they need God's love and healing. We are called to have a great amount of love and patience for these people keeping in mind that even some of the most hardened atheists have become believers in God.

Our job is to plant seeds and to pray that God waters them. In this conversation with a very cynical atheist, I feel many positive seeds were successfully planted. I know that he will think about the things we discussed, and who knows, maybe someday he will return to God. In addition, I was patient, loving, and kind, yet logical, confident, and a good example of Christ and Christianity. That is so important rather than speaking down to people in some sassy, judgmental way. I planted the seeds and prayed that God will do the rest. There is hope for *everyone* no matter how far gone!

# CHAPTER 6

✣

# If Jesus Isn't Real –
# Your Brain Isn't Either

### *An Exchange with an Outspoken Atheist*

---

<u>*Setting*</u>: *Seeing some students I knew in the cafeteria, I went over to say hello to them. As I did, a hostile atheist verbally assaulted me because of my belief in Jesus. He spoke fast and with an attitude. His tone was cynical and accusatory.*

Atheist:  Hey!  *You* believe in Jesus!

Me:  Yes.

Him:  *Why*?  You have absolutely *no proof* and therefore are brainwashed.

Me:  [Politely] Actually, there is *a lot* of proof.

Him:  Yeah right!  Give me one reason why you believe that

Jesus actually existed.

Me: The Bible.

Him: [Talking fast, like he's putting me on trial] Well, how do you *know* the Bible is true? Those are just stories. You have no *actual* proof. Let me put it to you this way. Have you seen Jesus?

Me: No.

Him: Have smelled Him?

Me: No.

Him: Have you touched Him?

Me: No.

Him: [Raising his voice] Then He's *not real*!! That much is clear, and therefore, you are brainwashed!

Me: Have you seen George Washington with your own eyes?

Him: [Without missing a beat] I've seen pictures of him.

Me: Let me put it to you this way: Have you seen your brain? Have you smelled it? And have you felt it?

Him: No, but I've seen pictures of my brain.

Me: No you haven't. Don't lie. And, even if you have seen your brain, I have not. And, since I have not personally seen your brain, smelled your brain, or felt your brain, then by your own logic, you don't have a brain, and it doesn't exist.

Him: That makes no sense. That's totally different.

Me: Actually, it makes perfect sense using your own logic. You said that because I have not seen, heard, smelled, or felt Jesus, then He's not real. I'm saying that I have also not seen, heard, smelled, or felt your brain, and therefore by the same reasoning, it's also not real.

Him: [Silent for a couple moments thinking] Good point! [Pause] But you're still brainwashed.

[Another student speaks up stating that he believes in Jesus]

Me: [To the student] Good for you, and virtually every history book, scholar, and encyclopedia in the history of the world agrees with you and me. Only a few people on the extreme fringe would argue that Jesus never existed.

Him: I could report you for talking about Jesus in school.

Me: [Without missing a beat] No you couldn't! *You* are the one who started the conversation. *You* are the one who attacked me for my beliefs. *You* are the one who asked *me* about Jesus in the first place, and I just answered your questions.

[The other students at the table all chime in]: Yeah, that is true.

*End Note:* All of the other students agreed with me, which brought the conversation to an end.

*Evangelization Note:* Another possible route this atheist could have taken in regard to his brain argument was to assert that scientific technology could help us to see our brains. Even though a person doesn't normally see the brain on a daily basis, it is *possible* to see the evidence of a brain using modern technology. In that case, I would probably mention the good evidence we possess for Jesus both in and out of the Bible that any honest person could observe and that archeology has confirmed over and over.

Alternatively, I could have chosen to bring up George Washington, the Holocaust, or any other figure or event from history. There are many people who believe that the Holocaust never happened. These people have "official signed" documents, pictures, and other "evidence" with which they make a very convincing case. Yet, the Holocaust happened. Thus, it would be necessary to examine all of the evidence, just like we would have to for Jesus and the Bible. Blindly rejecting and dismissing it because of a previous bias is not honest, intellectual, or helpful for dialogue.

# CHAPTER 7

✟

# Sex: Sports Car Or Old Van?

*Sexuality and True Love*

---

*Setting: One day, I had to teach a high school health class. The topic was "safe sex." Before leaving the classroom, the teacher informed the class that they would be watching an HIV video. She warned them that a woman "got AIDS because she was stupid and had casual sex." Then she told the class bluntly, "So, don't be stupid – use protection!" With that, she left the classroom.*

Naturally, I was disheartened over the fact that these teens were receiving such shallow information. Like a boxer waiting for the bell to ring, I could not wait for the video to be over so that I could give them the real truth about sex and love. Oddly, the video itself had nothing to do with "safe sex at all." Rather, it was about *abstinence* which completely contradicted everything the teacher had just said and which would work to my advantage. At the conclusion of the video, I summed up the important points and added my own thoughts. I began by saying, "There is no such thing as safe sex and no way to protect yourselves against some diseases by any contraceptive means."

Informing the class that the AIDS virus is smaller than the holes in the condom (which your teacher is telling you to use), I then added that the pill doesn't protect against AIDS or any other viruses at all. In fact, a man I knew from college read *the* authoritative study on condoms and HIV. In this study, it talked about a major condom conference that took place which gave a lot of information.

During the Q&A session, somebody asked the panel of people who made and promoted condoms if they themselves would use a condom if they *knew* their partner was infected with HIV. Not one of them raised their hand or said yes. Yet, health teachers are telling teens that this constitutes "safe sex." At this point, the class was listening intently. Even the trouble makers perked up and listened.

I went on to tell the class that there is no birth control that can protect against HPV (human papillomavirus – the most rampant of all diseases) nor other very common diseases. Without being tested, there is no way to know if you have contracted the virus because there are no signs or symptoms. HPV is the leading cause of cervical cancer in the country for women.[7]

---

[7] http://chastityproject.com/seminars/statistics/

I informed the class about a true story regarding a case where the husband had passed HPV to his wife unknowingly, who in turn passed it to their baby. Sadly, the baby has to get warts burned off her throat every month because her father slept around before marriage not did not consider any future consequences.

After letting that sink in for a second, I revealed that some diseases spread even without intercourse, through skin to skin contact. This is why diseases like HPV are spreading so rampantly.

Next, I called their attention to a part in the video which stated, "The only way *not* to get pregnant or to contract a disease is by practicing abstinence." While this is certainly true, people usually talk about the physical consequences of sex and rarely discuss the emotional and psychological consequences. So, I decided to emphasize one part of the video that showed a woman sticking tape to student's arms and ripping it off again. The woman did this to demonstrate the *emotional* consequences of sex.

"No one ever tells you that during sexual activity (not just sex but even hooking up), your brain releases powerful chemicals." I added, "One of these chemicals is oxytocin, the same chemical released between a mother and a baby. The purpose of this chemical is to strongly bond two people together."

If you stick tape to your arm and rip it off, it hurts a lot. It may even tear your hair out at the root. However, if you repeat this action multiple times, the tape loses its stick and its bonding ability, and it doesn't hurt any longer. It's the same with sexual activity before marriage and the release of oxytocin. The more sexual activity one engages in before marriage, the more a person loses their bonding ability, their ability to become intimate with another.

One reason for such rampant divorce in our country is that people have used up this 'stick' long before they are even married. They have given a piece of themselves away to this person, and to that person, and to that person over there, and to that person too, etc. What's left for their spouse? I once heard someone say that hooking up is like prostitution but without getting paid.[8]

I also told them that sleeping around and hooking up before marriage doesn't train you in discipline, faithfulness, self-control, and other things we need in order to have a happy and lasting marriage. In other words, they don't know what makes love work.

You may not get a disease having sex before marriage, but you might get a broken heart or the sad recognition that someone has taken something precious from you that you cannot get back. True abstinence is not just refraining from sex, but from *all sexual activity* until marriage, and honestly, you are all worth the wait.

"These are the negative side effects," I told them. "Focusing

---

[8] *Romance Without Regret*, by Jason and Crystalina Evert.

on them will only get you so far." "Therefore," I continued, "I would like to *focus on the positive* aspects of love and to inspire you to *want to wait for the highest love* once you see how important and beautiful true love is!"

Chastity is good, *very* good. Chastity is *not* a no but a *yes*. It says, yes I *can* have sex but with the *right person*, at the *right time*, in the *right place*, in the *right way* (i.e. with your spouse, in marriage, and for the sake of true love).

I then asked the class, "Are you worth the wait? Remember, every one of you is a prince or a princess and deserve to be treated as such." Then I gave them an analogy.[9] Some people view their sexuality as a rusty broken down van. The seats are ripped and the dashboard is cracked. Even the rear view mirrors and bumpers have fallen off. The owners don't even lock the van in parking lots because they don't care if anyone steals it. In other words, it's not worth much or anything at all to them.

On the other hand, there are people who view their sexuality as a new beautiful sports car which has a very expensive alarm system. The alarm is not because the car is dirty or bad but precisely because it's so good, beautiful, expensive, and worth protecting. Someday, the owner of this fancy car will open up the untarnished driver side door and let their soulmate into the passenger seat. Head over heels in love,

---

[9] The following analogy comes from a book called, "The Incredible Gift," by Keith and Tami Kiser.

they will take a ride together to happily-ever-after and share that intimate journey together for life.

How do *you* view yourself and your sexuality? As a rusty old van that's not worth much or anything at all? You'll let others hook up with you and use you because you don't see much worth or value in yourself or your body. Or, do you see yourself as a beautiful sports car? You recognize that your body and your sexuality are beautiful, valuable, and worth *so* much that you can't even put a price on them.

I concluded; "How do you see yourselves? As a cheap date or as a soulmate? It doesn't matter what you have been in the past, it matters who you want to be in the future. What kind of love do you desire and what kind of lover do you *wish* to be?"

*End Note:* As I concluded my speech, a number of students in the class erupted with a vigorous applause. They were smiling widely and beaming with joy from this message. They all thanked me for speaking to them about this and went on to talk about it among themselves as the bell rang.

*An important note about starting over:* If there was more time, I would have liked to inform the class that it is never too late to start over again or to regain their purity. Many teens relish this message of true love when it's put to them in a way they can understand, and they even desire it in their own lives. With that being said, some teens (and adults) have made mistakes along the way or are currently in bad relationships. Some feel used. Others feel like damaged goods. Others know they are being used and recognize that the van analogy applies to them. Thus, there are people who believe that because they've messed up, it is too late for them. But, that is not true.

I always try to make it a point to tell both teens and adults (anyone at all) that it is never too late to start over. I offer the famous example of a $20 bill. When the teens are asked who would like to have the bill for free, most hands go right up. Then, I crumple the $20 bill into a ball and ask, "Who wants it now?" The hands stay up. Next, I throw the crumpled bill on the ground and step on it a few times. After picking it up again I ask, "Does anyone still want it?" All of the hands reach up higher.

The point here is that no matter how crumpled the bill is, it's still $20. Likewise, we are not our mistakes, and we have a worth that goes far beyond our dirt. We are still us, and we are *priceless*. We are always worthy of love because we are sons and daughters of God. It is never too late to start over to become the person that God made us to be. The best part of all is that God will be there all along the way to help us.

Whereas there is roughly a 70% divorce rate for people who sleep together before marriage, anyone who chooses to start over and save themselves for marriage[10] triple their odds of

---

[10] Waiting until marriage is not just waiting to have sex. It's saving your *whole self* including your body for your future spouse. Therefore, we gladly refrain from hooking up and all sexual activity for the sake of this higher love in marriage.

marital success and happiness. So, it makes sense to start again.

Our sexuality can be likened to a bank account that has been decreased or even drained due to excessive sexual activity. We are supposed to save our money (our gift of sexuality) for our future spouse, but we have made some poor choices. The best thing a person can do is to make a concrete decision to start saving that money again.

In other words, I challenge people to make the commitment to save themselves for marriage, to pray, go to confession, and to write a letter to their future spouse telling them of their new commitment for the sake of true love.

Going to confession and giving your past to God is the best way to start over! You must let Him forgive you, cleanse you, heal you, and make you new. Remember, only God can write straight with all of the crooked lines we have made in our life. Not only *can* He help you start over, He *wants* to! Moreover, God can help you to forgive *yourself* too!

Countless people have started over and made a "secondary virginity" pledge. They have found both love and happiness, and you can too! It's never too late. But, it all starts with a *decision* to do that. Pray for yourself and for your future husband or wife. Pray that God will make you as white as the whitest snow. It may be a journey, but every road to new life and every mountaintop experience is always more than worth the wait!

✠

# CHAPTER 8

# Why Would God Send Us To Hell?

## *A Conversation on Sin, Eternity, the Existence of God, and more*

---

*Setting: I once overheard a Christian trying to explain God to an atheist and having a difficult time doing so. Naturally, I decided to join the conversation.*

Atheist: That's so stupid, I don't believe that!

Me: What's so stupid if you don't mind me asking?

Him: I don't believe in the Christian God because if you do the slightest little sin you're going to end up in hell. You pretty much can't do *anything* or you're going to hell.

Me: That's actually a misconception and not an accurate portrayal of Christianity or God at all. You're representing God only through the eyes of vengeance. But, that is not who He is. Think about it this way. My wife and I have a wonderful relationship, but I'm not always perfect. I am sometimes impatient, stubborn, angry, and I often have to apologize to her for the silly things I do.

Now, she doesn't just immediately divorce me because I mess up or make a mistake. With that being said, if I started drinking and abusing her or beating her over a long period of time, or if I was cheating on her; those are tougher bridges to cross and may not be reconcilable (though perhaps they could be if I repented, was truly sorry, and set about to change those actions for good).

It is the same with God. I sin many times a day, every day. Everyone does. Yet, these sins do not break my relationship with God. I'm not intentionally trying to sin, I'm just imperfect and make mistakes. Yet, God still loves me with an infinite love. However, if one of my sins is particularly evil, and if I *know* it's evil, and I still choose to do it anyway, that's a much harder bridge to cross. When we sin like that, we are actually making the choice to push God away telling Him in effect to, "Get out of my life."

If you found out your best friend on earth stole $1,000 from your family, would you still be friends with him? Probably not. But did you break the friendship? No, he did through his actions. It's the same with sin, the bigger the sin, the more we push God away. With that being said, even if I break my relationship with Him by my own choice, He will always forgive me if I apologize and set about to change for the better. The best part is that He actually *wants* to forgive us because there is nothing more important to Him than a relationship with His children.

Him: Yes, OK, but God still sends people to hell.

Me: More truthfully, we send ourselves the hell by the choices we make and the way we act. It's *our* choice. My wife may divorce me if I beat her again and again, but it's my own actions which caused the divorce and not her final decision to protect herself by separating from me.

If I truly loved her, I would show it in my actions. In contrast, if I merely say I love her but continue to hurt her, then my words are a lie. I don't actually love her, and the divorce is the result of that. Through my own actions, I chose to destroy the marriage. I could have had a happy marriage with her but chose the opposite.

The Catholic Church teaches that only those who *freely reject God* go to hell. Take one extreme example: angry atheist Christopher Hitchens. Mr. Hitchens even on his deathbed fiercely rejected God and stated that *even if* God appeared to him, he would never believe or want to go to heaven. What can God do about that? God is not going to grab Christopher by the shirt collar, shake him, and then throw him roughly into heaven against his will.

God gave us all the free will to choose. So, if Mr. Hitchens chooses not to live with God, then even though that breaks God's heart, He will honor and respect that. Since Mr. Hitchens wants nothing to do with God and does not want

God in His life, He will go the place where there is no God – Hell. That's what Hell is; it's the complete absence of God.

Of course, God doesn't *want* anyone to go to Hell, which is why He came into the world in the first place in the person of Jesus Christ. Jesus was innocent, loving, and compassionate. He did miracles and forgave people's sins. Yet, then He was tortured and hung on a cross for us in order to forgive our sins and those of the whole world. The Roman cross was one of the most brutal torture devices, and Jesus chose to go through it to pay the price for our sins so we could go to heaven. What else could God do to show us His love?

Him: [Thinking about it for a split second] That makes a little sense. [Thinks on it some more] But there is still no proof for God.

Me: There is proof for God's existence.

Him: Scientific proof?

Me: No, not scientific proof. How could there be? God transcends the universe (is far beyond all created material things) meaning that science does not remotely have the capability to detect Him. What is science after all?

Science is the empirical study of the *natural* world. Science deals with what can be seen, observed, and tested through hypothesis and repeated experiment. Since God is spirit (supernatural) and cannot be seen or tested for by any natural means, science is not the answer. It doesn't work in the realm of the supernatural and is therefore insufficient in trying to prove or disprove God.

Some people claim that everything must to be proven by science in order to believe it. However, science cannot prove everything and never will be able to. It is not the be-all and end-all of proof. Science is generally limited to its own field. There are some questions that only mathematics can answer in its own perspective field, for example.

There's a theory out now about a possible multi-universe, but science is not advanced enough to prove this and may never be. While it may be true, we would not have the ability to prove it for a very long time, if ever. So, if science can't even prove all natural questions right now, how could it seriously intend on answering supernatural ones?

For proof, just look at the universe. For thousands of years, most everybody believed that the universe was eternal and that it went back forever. Most Christians disagreed, stating that it had a definite beginning. They were often ridiculed and persecuted. However, in the 1920s with the discovery of the Big Bang, it demonstrated that the universe had a definite beginning. Time, space, matter and energy all were shown to have a distinct beginning just as Christians said.[11] Now even

---

[11] St. Thomas Aquinas was one of the top minds in the history of the Catholic Church. He is known for his famous, "Five Proofs for the Existence of God." Many people don't realize that Aquinas' arguments take into account the possibility of an infinite universe (if that is, in fact, true). If the universe is eternal, far from disproving God, Aquinas

if there are countless other universes which have preceded our own, by what we know of mathematics today, material things can go back indefinitely. Thus, everything would have to arrive at a first cause eventually.

Think about this: if there were an infinite amount of days in the past, then there would *always* be an *infinite* amount of days before today, and therefore we would *never reach today*. Infinity would always make it impossible to ever arrive at today. However, we are here at today, and so there could not have been an infinite amount of time in the past. Consequently, there had to be someone or something which transcends the universe, God or something else, something that is not dependent on anything else for existence and is the cause of everything else. This first mover who got everything started is the first cause. This is what Christians call God.

Scientifically, everything that *comes into existence* has a *cause* – a reason why it exists. What is the cause for all created reality and material existence? Christians say that cause is God who is the first Cause, the one who didn't need to be caused but is the cause of everything else.

Matter can't be the cause of the material universe because matter cannot be the cause of itself. It's the same for every other dead, non-transcendent thing. There had to be someone

---

accounted for this in his proofs and easily harmonized it with the existence of God show how God would still be the necessary cause of all.

who is the original cause of everything who transcends our temporal reality.

As I said already, it cannot be matter since matter had a beginning. Thus, God cannot be made out of matter, but must be spiritual in nature. Since time and space came into existence and had a beginning, God cannot be in time or space but transcends them – meaning He is timeless (eternal) and spaceless (immaterial). And that which caused everything to be must be extremely intelligent and very powerful. Sounds a lot like the Christian definition of God. While you may choose not to believe this, one cannot say there isn't *any* evidence for God.

*End Note:* At this point, the atheist became lost in thought for a while. Later on, I came back and complemented him for his desire to seek the truth, to research different beliefs, and to wrestle with these questions.

*Evangelization Note:* The need to clear up people's misconceptions is a must. This atheist was far more open when he understood what Christians actually taught. He was far more inclined to believe when the faith was presented to him in a logical manner that he could understand. For this to happen, we need to know and understand our own faith and have the ability to explain it. Perhaps consider reading these conversations a few times until the information sinks in. That way you can use this knowledge when the time comes… and it will at some point.

# CHAPTER 9

✝

# Religion Has *Faith* – Science Has *Facts*

### *A Conversation about God, Evolution, and other Religious Questions*

---

<u>Setting</u>: *An atheist and I had a delightful and friendly discussion about everything under the sun. For those who are unfamiliar with Richard Dawkins (mentioned in this conversation), he is one of the chief atheists in the world leading the war against religion and trying to destroy people's faith. He is aggressive, insulting, controversial, and often offensive, looking down on people of religion.*

Atheist: Have you watched any good debates recently? I recently saw one with Richard Dawkins against a Catholic Bishop.

Me: Yeah, I saw that one too. While not perfect, I thought that the bishop did a pretty good job and held his own.

Him: I thought he did a really poor job and didn't explain anything.

Me: Funny, that's how I felt about Richard Dawkins. To me, Dawkins just spoke nonsense. Many of the things he said were so... odd. In fact, you probably remember the couple of times in the debate that the audience actually laughed out loud at some of the things he said.

Him: Yeah, I remember that.

Me: Now, I've watched a lot of debates, and I personally have never seen an audience laugh at someone like that. To me, it shows how nonsensical some of his arguments were. This is ironic since Dawkins attempts to come across as intellectually superior compared to religious people. Yet, his arguments are not that intellectual. They are far more emotional.

Him: Why do you say that? Can you give me an example?

Me: I recently read his book, *The God Delusion*, and it was monumentally disappointing. This book has been touted as *the* book to destroy faith and religion. Naturally, I thought it would be a good challenge to my faith. However, throughout the book, I just kept saying, "Is that it? Are these *really* his best arguments?" Honestly, I was blown away at how shallow and unconvincing his arguments were, which is one reason why many of his fellow atheists have distanced themselves from him and are embarrassed by many of his arguments.

Him:  I don't always like Dawkins either, but I thought that some of his opinions in the book were presented well.  What specifically did you not like about his arguments?

Me:  That is a good question.  For starters, one of my biggest problems is the blatant and obvious bias that he comes to the table with along with his flagrantly dishonest presentation of the facts.  Most times, *Dawkins does not even get the Christian argument correct* before he begins tearing apart what wasn't true in the first place.  I think a person should understand the other side's beliefs before attacking them falsely.  Secondly, his arguments are so extreme.  They're like a constant hyperbole that can hardly be taken seriously.

Him:  What do you mean?

Me:  In his chapter on morality, Dawkins uses the example of *one* man who shot an abortion doctor back in *1994* (20+ years ago) and then uses this one person over several pages to prove that *all religion* is bad.  Can you see how that doesn't follow?  One confused man equals all religion?

In like manner, he then proceeds to conjure up a few extremists like Osama Bin Laden in attempts to prove that *all* religion is evil and must be eradicated.  To me, it's wholeheartedly dishonest to use a handful of extremists to then assert that millions, even billions of normal everyday Christians and religious people are like that – or "would be if they were allowed."

Wouldn't you agree that the majority of religious people are normal and not anything like Osama Bin Laden? Many work in hospitals, day care centers, and nursing homes; they do service and social work and try to make the world a better place. Dawkins will claim that one religious person started a war and go on to conclude that religion is the cause of all war. Honestly, his arguments are so extreme and too shallow to even be taken seriously.

Him: Well, religion has started a lot of wars. Look at the Crusades or the wars that are going on today in the name of religion. The way I see it is that people have fought over beliefs for thousands of years. There was much intolerance. Every religion thought they had a monopoly on the truth, and they couldn't tolerate others who disagreed with them.

Then science came along and gave us facts instead of mere belief. Science has provided answers for many things we never knew or were ignorant about. I feel that the more we know about the world, and the more we possess the facts to back it up, the less superstition there will be. Also, the more educated and informed we become, the less violent mankind seems to be. To me, science is the answer we are looking for, not religion.

Me: It is true that religion has been the cause of some wars. However, that's a far cry from asserting that religion is the cause of *all war* and *all violence* in the world. It's not like non-believers are more evolved or any less violent. Why doesn't Dawkins mention atheists like Joseph Stalin who killed 20 million of his own people, or the atheist Mao in China who killed 70 million of his own people, or Pol Pot who wiped out 1/5 of his own countries' population, just for example?

Many argue that Hitler was an atheist (at the least, he wasn't religious for most of his life), and he wiped out about 10 million people. Hitler alone killed more than the Crusades, the Inquisition, and all other religious wars combined, not to mention Stalin, Mao, and all the other atheists![12] I wonder why Dawkins conveniently overlooks all of these facts. Worse, he goes to great lengths to excuse them. It's dishonest at best.

Moreover, non-believers and skeptics almost always turn a blind eye to *all the good religion has done*. For example, the Catholic Church is the largest charitable organization in the world. That's a fact! The Catholic Church founded hospitals, orphanages, and homes to help people; they work to stop drug trafficking, violence, injustice, and countless other things. No one feeds more people, clothes more people, or helps more people around the world than the Catholic Church.

Him: That is true. I agree with that. The Catholic Church does do a lot of good. But Christians through the centuries have done a lot of bad too. You can't deny that! They've killed many people in the name of religion. Heck, they used to burn each other at the stake, and I don't even have to mention the atrocity of the Salem Witch Trials.

---

[12] D'Souza, Dinesh, *What's So Great About Christianity*, chapter 5.

Me: Before I address that, we must remember a few things. First, as I just stated, the Catholic Church is the largest charitable organization in the world doing more good than anyone else on the planet including atheists. I think atheists need to recognize that. In general, I don't think non-believers give the Church any credit where credit is due.

Allow me to digress for a minute on this topic that will help illustrate my point. The Catholic Church gets a lot of criticism for the "Dark Ages" even though the Church had nothing to do with these times being dark. One main reason the Dark Ages were so horrific is because of all the barbarian tribes that attacked and destroyed the Roman Empire for hundreds of years. The Huns, Danes, Goths, Visigoths, and the Vikings (to name a few) crashed upon the Roman Empire and laid waste to it again and again.

During that time though, the Catholic Church was a bright light shining in the darkness! The Church saved all of Western Civilization in many ways. For example, the Church saved literacy. When one library was destroyed by the barbarians, the monks traveled quickly to another monastery to begin re-copying the books. They even copied the classics, classics that we would not have today if it were not for the Catholic Church. In fact, learning might have been lost for ages were it not for the monks keeping literacy alive.

It's also important to realize that it was the *Catholic Church* who invented the *university* system. We attend universities today thanks to the Church. This debunks the myth that the Church was against learning or that intellectual growth was at a standstill during the Middle Ages.

Quite the opposite. The Catholic Church also invented law, economics, and many other things that we take for granted today in the United States. The Catholic Church even taught science in the universities for centuries, and it was all of the scientific study in and out of these universities that made the scientific revolution later on even possible.[13]

The Church also invented the scientific method. Popes and countless other priests esteemed science to the highest. In fact, Galileo, Copernicus, Fr. Roger Bacon, Gregor Mendel, Blaise Pascal, Isaac Newton, Fr. Boskovich, Fr. George Lemaitre, and countless others all practiced science and contributed in large ways to scientific advancement. So while religion certainly has done some bad things, the Catholic Church has done infinitely more good than bad.

Him: That mostly makes sense to me. You are right that the Church has done a lot of good. But you mentioned Galileo; what about Galileo? The Catholic Church persecuted him because he was getting too close to the truth. They arrested him, sent him to the Inquisition, locked him up, and prevented him from practicing science. Scientific reality was beginning to disprove what the Catholic Church had held true for so long but could not prove. The Church felt threatened by that. So, they arrested Galileo and put him in prison.

---

[13] Information in this particular paragraph came from the book, *How the Catholic Church Built Western Civilization*, by Thomas E. Woods.

Me: If you don't mind, I'd like to come back to that in a minute. I'd like to finish my train of thought regarding the good things that religion has done in order to completely dispel the myth that religion is all about war and violence as Dawkins and other atheists continually assert.

One other thing I was about to mention is that the Catholic Church sent missionaries into the world to lovingly and peacefully share the Catholic faith. Here's a fun fact. No army on earth could conquer the barbarian tribes in the Middle Ages, not even the mighty Roman Empire. In the end, it was the Catholic Church who civilized them by preaching the Gospel of Jesus Christ.

In fact, it was also Christianity who civilized the cannibals over in the area of Oceania. Nations of cannibals don't eat people anymore *because of Christianity* who civilized them with the saving message of Jesus Christ. The Church has done *so* much good, and has undeniably made the world a better place. Atheists are ignorant about a lot of these things, or they conveniently overlook them all.

Him: You're right. Christians have done a lot of good. But still, what about the Crusades? Wasn't that just a big power grab by the Church? I mean, you have all of these religions fighting for the Holy Land. You have Muslims who disagreed with the Catholic Church. The Jews were disagreeing too. Muslims and Jews were both persecuted by the Catholic Church, no? The Crusades alone prove that the Church was intolerant and bloodthirsty for power over many centuries.

People have fought over their beliefs for thousands of years. There was a lot of intolerance because people didn't have the facts of science. I mean, we used to think the earth was the center of the universe, and the Church held that belief until science disproved it. I would assert that the more sophisticated we get, and the more science clears away past ignorance, the better this world will be. Maybe it would be best if we all forget religion and just focused on science. What would you say to that?

Me: Well, as I stated earlier, the Catholic Church which *is* a religion helped civilize the world and make it better. That was all without modern science. Catholics still do more good for the world than any and all scientists today. So, I don't think that argument holds up. Secondly, atheists lump all religions together into one category without distinction.

They blame "religion" for being the source of all conflict and violence. But not all religions can be put in the same category because most religions are not violent by nature; Buddhism for example. Even religions that have had some violence vary drastically in regard to the amount.

Statistically, over 90% of wars fought in the last century were by Muslims against other Muslims or against non-Muslims. So, while this may demonstrate that Islam is a violent religion, it does not prove that *all* religions act this way. They do not. In fact, the Crusades (which everyone attacks but few understand) were wars of self-defense *against* the savage Muslims. Islam was violent from its outset, and Christianity eventually decided to defend herself against the attackers.

Every historian knows that Muhammad was kicked out of Mecca for preaching his new religion and fled to Medina where he raised an army. He then returned to Mecca and razed the city to the ground. Thereafter, his new army gathered strength and went on to conquer the entire surrounding area. By the time Muhammad died, he had conquered the whole area of land we know today as the "Fertile Crescent."

After Muhammad's death, Islam grew even more rapidly. From 657 A.D. to 757 A.D, the armies of Islam conquered everything from Afghanistan to North Africa. Next, they invaded Europe and conquered many islands. In a short span of time, Islam conquered the Persian Empire, the Roman Empire, and two-thirds of the Byzantine Empire, which was the last major empire on earth – centuries of war without batting an eye. What did the Catholic Church do in response? Nothing. The pope and the Church prayed for the Muslims for centuries hoping it would all stop. In other words, the Church always responded with non-violence.

Him: I think I've heard pieces of that before. You put it all in perspective though, and that makes more sense.

Me: You've heard that before? Well, you are one of the rare few. One of the big myths of history is that the Crusades were just intolerant wars by a power-hungry church that just desired money or persecuted anyone who wasn't Catholic. With all of this as a backdrop though, anyone can see why the Crusades we called. It was because the powerful Muslim armies were devastating the world and the Byzantine Empire. In fact, Commodore Alexius I who had been at odds with the pope, decided to humble himself and ask the pope and the Catholic Church for help.

The pope prayed about it for a long time and eventually decided to come to the aid of his "brothers in need." That was the chief reason the Crusades were called – to help their Byzantine brothers and sisters. In addition to that, more than half of all Christian lands had been overrun by Islamic armies. From time to time, thousands of innocent and unarmed Christians were massacred by Muslims while on pilgrimage to Jerusalem. Something needed to be done.

Thus, the Crusades were finally called to help answer the call of the Byzantine Emperor, to retake the Holy Land and protect innocent pilgrims traveling there, and to help Christians around the world who were suffering and dying. The Crusades were wars of self-defense and were rooted in a noble cause. Unlike Islam, Christianity had been a mostly peaceful religion and had done more good for the world than anyone else. I'm not saying that Christians were perfect through the centuries or that bad things did not happen during the Crusades, but extreme abuses were not the norm. They were the exception.

Him: I still think we should just look to science. I can understand that not all religions are violent, but still, some are. Science gives us the answers we need and have sought for thousands of years. We used to believe in gods and goddesses and that Zeus would zap you if you disobeyed him. But nobody believes that anymore. God is becoming increasingly more irrelevant as science progresses.

There were many things that science has proven that the Church did not and could not know. There was a blank slate of information you might say. Their attempt at knowledge was just to insert "God" into any answer they did not know. Then science comes along with actual evidence. Look at evolution. The Church taught that everyone came from Adam and Eve Who God created, but then Darwin came along and undid thousands of years of belief. We know that the Catholic Church even tried to stop scientific progress because they were threatened by it.

Me: First of all, not everyone believed in the Greek gods. That was only one area of the world. Secondly, as I've demonstrated, the Catholic Church has never been against science. While some Christians certainly are today, it's a misconception to claim that the Catholic Church just filled in unknown gaps with "God." Catholics actually taught real science both in labs and in the colleges and universities they started. Did you know that it was the Catholic Church that invented the scientific method?

Also, it was a *Catholic priest* who first discovered and outlined the theory of the *Big Bang*. As I already mentioned, many of the greatest mathematicians and scientists on earth were Catholic including popes and priests. So, how could the Church have been against science all while practicing and promoting it? Heck, we wouldn't even have science to study and talk about today if it wasn't for the Catholic Church in the first place.

See, you assume that people of old just sat around with empty heads waiting for science to come, but the complete opposite is true. For the Catholic Church, it isn't *either* God *or* science, it's *both*. In fact, it was Christianity's belief in God as Creator that sparked their desire to venture out and learn more about the universe God created. So, you are creating a false dichotomy between the Church and science, one that does not really exist.

Him: Then why did the Catholic Church persecute Galileo? As I already mentioned, they sent him to the Inquisition because his science disproved the Church's long held theories. Also, why did the Church reject Darwin? Darwin proved that history and religious belief were wrong regarding how life came about.

Unlike religion that just relies on its holy books for truth but has no evidence, Darwin had actual, verifiable proof. Naturally, he was persecuted for it by those in authority who kept their people in darkness. Maybe it was because they did not want to lose their positions of power.

What religious people held for thousands and thousands of years, Darwin reversed in decades of scientific discovery. Yet, how many religious people ignore science and just continue to blindly follow their holy books. They even follow it against sound reason and logic. Case and point:

"Creationism."[14]  Belief in creationism is anti-science.

Me: The Bible when it is properly understood does not contradict science at all.  And to my knowledge, the Catholic Church has never been against evolution or science.  You may be thinking of Protestant Christians.  Protestants who believe in Creationism and accept a literal interpretation of the Bible certainly reject evolution.  But not all Protestant Christians do, and the Catholic Church certainly does not. But about Galileo; the Catholic Church did not condemn him for scientific reasons.

Him: What?  Of course they did.  They didn't like what he was teaching.  Religious people have always condemned things they don't understand or that threaten their beliefs. People of religion thought they were so special because of their belief that they were the "center of the universe." However, that was until science came along and showed us the truth.  The reality is that we are nothing but an infinitesimal speck in the midst of millions of universes.  The universes are literally unmeasurable.  So why do you think that we who are smaller than dust are so special?

---

[14] Creationism is a belief within some circles of Christianity – usually in Protestant circles.  It asserts that the universe is only about 6,000 years old and that creation was accomplished in seven literal days.  Creationists are skeptical of secular scientific findings and reject the theory of evolution.  Many would even go so far as to say that evolution is evil and from the devil.  There is a wide range of belief within Creationism ranging from moderate to staunch.  The Catholic Church does not accept Creationism though some individual Catholics might.  Christians who reject science and preach Creationism can give the rest of Christianity a bad name.

Me: First, regarding Galileo, you have to understand that the Catholic Church was not alone in being suspicious of this new theory. Virtually *everyone* was, including non-religious scientists. This was because geocentricity (the idea that the earth was the center of the universe) had been taught for nearly 2000 years and virtually without question.

In fact, neither Galileo nor Copernicus were the first to propose that theory. People back at the time of Aristotle first suggested it. However, Aristotle and Ptolemy demolished every argument so thoroughly that nobody really questioned it again until Copernicus. Geocentricity became the norm, the accepted truth throughout the world both in and out of the Church.

Nicolaus Copernicus, a Catholic priest and a renowned scientist, emerged onto the scene. He discovered evidence that seemed to overturn this ancient belief. Copernicus worked hard and wrote extensively on the topic but was hesitant to publish his work.

However, bishops and Jesuits within the Catholic Church prodded him and finally convinced him to publish his great work called, *On the Revolution of the Heavenly Spheres*. He dedicated his work to the *Pope*! This validates the fact that the Church and the pope were *not* against his theory or science in general.

It was a *Catholic* scientist who discovered heliocentricity (the notion that the sun is at the center of the universe and the earth and planets revolve around the sun). So you can't keep promoting the false dichotomy that it's either the Church or science as if they have been enemies for all of history.

On the contrary, this is typical of how science and religion have worked together in harmony for much of history. Johannes Kepler would add to Copernicus' work on heliocentricity, and the Church supported him too.

The Catholic Church was not against Galileo either for continuing to work on this theory. Heliocentricity is not what got Galileo in trouble. In fact, you might be surprised to know that the pope, the Jesuits, and the Catholic Church in general loved Galileo and his scientific work. The Jesuits (a highly educated order of priests within the Catholic Church) even *funded his research.*

Why would they do that if the Church was against science? The Jesuits even threw huge celebrations in honor of Galileo and all his accomplishments.[15] In fact, three consecutive popes showered praises upon Galileo and his works, including the current pope at the time, Pope Urban VIII who was his friend. That's no small thing. So, you're probably wondering what happened.

Since geocentricity was an accepted fact in most everyone's

---

[15] Remember that at least 35 craters on the moon were named after Jesuit priests because they so dominated scientific research and discovery throughout the Middle Ages. These were mammoth scientists and intellectuals who supported Galileo and his work.

minds, and since the Church was funding Galileo, they wanted him to have enough actual evidence to overturn 2000 years of accepted "fact." The Church was not necessarily against heliocentricity per say, but against promoting it as a fact before it could be proven as such. In other words, they wanted it treated *as a theory* until enough evidence could be garnered to overturn any previous belief. In this way, the Church was acting very scientifically.

This is exactly what Copernicus did, which is why he didn't find himself in hot water. He treated heliocentricity *as a theory*. The problem with Galileo is that he jumped to conclusions he couldn't sufficiently prove at the time. Many of his assertions and theories would not be fully demonstrated or verified until decades after his death when technology would become advanced enough to make it conclusive.

Galileo often got ahead of himself in his claims and ignored the warnings. He began to teach heliocentricity as a fact – even before he could prove it. This became the beginning of his problems, and he was sent to the Inquisition. While it might seem like the Church was against science here, the opposite is actually true.

This is proven by the fact that the *pope* himself came to visit Galileo and personally asked him to reopen his study on heliocentricity. As friends, they debated with each other in good spirit. The pope offered the accepted arguments of the day in order to hear the discoveries and findings Galileo was coming up with. In the end, the pope liked what Galileo had to say and gave him permission to continue working on it. However, the pope strongly cautioned him to treat heliocentricity as a theory until he possessed enough evidence to prove this new model of the universe.

Thus, it was at the urging of the pope that Galileo wrote the *Dialogue on the Great World Systems*.[16] Galileo penned this book as a dialogue between two people. One of the persons was an enlightened intellectual who gave arguments in favor of heliocentricity.

The other person in the book was uneducated and naïve, holding on to an outmoded way of thinking. Galileo had used the conversations with the pope he had as material for his book. Unfortunately, he made the uneducated character in the book to represent the pope and many of the Jesuits. Naturally, this angered and alienated the very people who supported and funded him. The pope and the Jesuits were not amused by Galileo's insults and reacted poorly.

Galileo may have survived this great insult, but then he went further and stepped over the line by venturing outside the boundaries of being a scientist. He began to speak as a theologian and to pronounce that the Bible was wrong on

---

[16] Again, this is certainly proof that the Church was not against science. If they were, the pope would have never let Galileo begin working on anything scientific ever again. This event shows that the Church actually liked him and encouraged his work. Anyone interested in this topic may wish to read the book, *Galileo's Daughter*. This has some actual letters between Galileo and his daughters which reveal a much different story than the commonly believed myths many hold today.

certain verses. This is something neither Copernicus nor Kepler ever dared to do. *That* is the big thing that got him in trouble.

The pope and the Jesuits took his insults personally. Galileo seemed to have a gift for alienating the people around him, the very people who were trying to help him. This is when the Church stepped in and put an end to his work on that specific subject.

We know that the pope did not merely reprimand him or communicate his disappointment but stopped his work altogether.[17] Galileo was sent to the Inquisition to be tried. The Inquisitions were good and fair state-run courts, probably the fairest courts of the day. Galileo was finally forced to recant. But again, this was mainly for his condemnation of certain Biblical passages and a refusal to submit to the Church in that regard. It was not a condemnation of heliocentricity, though that was a side effect of the Church's overreaction to the situation.

Contrary to popular belief, Galileo was never imprisoned or tortured. Rather he was placed under house arrest in a beautiful palace with all the latest amenities and even his own personal butlers – again demonstrating that the Church was not against science. Galileo *was allowed to* continue his scientific studies and his work. Ironically, Galileo's greatest

---

[17] Something Pope John Paul II would apologize for centuries later. He apologized for how the Church handled, or rather mishandled, the situation.

scientific achievements came during his time under house arrest. In the end, Galileo died in good graces with the Church and *both of his daughters became nuns!*

So, in summary, the Church was correct in being cautious with this new theory and for desiring sufficient scientific proof for it, but they reacted excessively and emotionally. No one doubts that they mishandled the matter.

Sorry! That was such a long explanation, but few people realize what actually happened. So, I just wanted to put it all into the proper perspective.

Him: [Silently thinking about it all for a little while] Hmm, that's interesting. I didn't know about the whole daughters becoming nuns thing.

Me: Yes, it's true.

Him: [Thinking deeply for a little while more] Well, what about Darwin? What does the Catholic Church think about that? From what I hear, Intelligent Design people believe that complexity proves God. They can't understand how an eye ball, the human body, or the complexity of life could have arisen without God.

However, because of science we see more clearly and accurately now. We understand that it was evolution which allowed these things to develop – and without God. So many religious people condemn evolution and refuse to accept it because it contradicts their religion.

Me: I can see where you are coming from, but I would caution you to be careful in your conclusions. Yes, evolution may be true, but we don't (and could not) know for sure scientifically speaking, that God had no hand in it, even if all He did was to get it started.

In fact, this is one subject Darwin himself hardly touched. He couldn't (and science still cannot) explain how we got life from non-living matter. Everything was dead. Then somehow we just got life one day. There may be a natural explanation for it, or there may not be. But if you look at Darwin's tree of life and trace it back to the base, to the very first living organism, one must ask, what was before that? How did life arise from non-living matter?

If we go further back than that, why does anything exist at all rather than just nothing? See, evolution could only take place because things already existed that made it possible. If those things never existed in the first place, evolution could not have happened.

Him: Yes, but evolution does explain everything.

Me: No offense, but it doesn't explain everything including how we got life from non-life or where everything came from in the first place. By definition, evolution can only explain how life evolved, not how it was initially started. It also cannot explain the complexity of DNA.

The DNA strand itself (represented by the letters ATCG) tells amino acids and proteins how to build life. One strand of DNA in a human being needs *3 billion* letters of ATCG repeated endlessly in different combinations. Imagine dumping Scrabble letters out of a bag onto the floor and trying to spell out a Shakespeare play. Each one of those letters would have to fall into place randomly and perfectly millions of times over. People used to think this kind of accidental causality could happen.

I'm sure you have heard of the experiment employing many monkeys to bang randomly on computer keyboards all day long. Scientists thought that with enough time, monkeys could eventually produce something coherent and similar to Shakespeare. However, the more they typed, the more gibberish was produced – hour after hour, day after day, year after year. They randomly hit the keys but did not produce Shakespeare or anything discernibly recognizable. So, scientists need to explain how all the letters came together randomly to create the DNA, which is the most complex set of information in all of the known universes.

Even if human DNA evolved, the very first *un-evolved* organism still possessed hundreds of typed pages of DNA code which needs explanation. Imagine over one hundred thousand letters of ATCG over and over again in seemingly endless combinations. Evolution cannot explain that complexity because it was in the first un-evolved organism.

Him: Not yet, but science will figure it out someday.

Me: Maybe. Maybe not. Even if they do find a natural explanation, it still doesn't prove that God didn't have anything to do with it or design it that way. If God is real, He would have absolutely had a hand in making everything even if He didn't micromanage each and every step.

Fun fact: you might be surprised to know that Charles Darwin did not invent the theory of evolution, and that there were two other "co-founders" of evolution who were far smarter than Darwin who are rarely talked about. These two other scientists both accepted that God had a hand in the evolutionary process.

Him: What are you even talking about? Darwin didn't invent evolution? Come on.

Me: It's true. Charles Darwin didn't invent the theory, and the Galapagos Islands that he traveled to were not a chance discovery. It's a fact that Darwin's grandfather, *Erasmus Darwin*, taught and wrote extensively about the theory of evolution long before Charles was even born. He even wrote a book on the topic called *Zoonomia*. Charles had read this book and others on the subject, and it created a great excitement in him. In fact, the very reason he travelled to the Galapagos Islands was to continue his grandfather's research.

Him: I have *never* heard of such a thing and don't know anyone else who has either.

Me: Well, you told me that you had heard the Crusades were wars of self-defense against the ravaging Muslim armies. The vast majority of society doesn't know anything about this fact but has bought into myths about the Crusades.

Another myth many people accept today is that those who lived in the Middle Ages all believed the earth was flat. This has been taught in schools for a very long time but is finally being reversed.

I work in the public schools, and I myself have seen the history books finally being revised and rewritten to correct this error. Yet, people all over the country continue to accept and repeat this myth. The bottom line is that there are many false stories we have been taught. Charles Darwin inventing evolution is just one of them.

Him: Yes, but everyone knows Darwin invented evolution.

Me: Do we? Let me ask you a question then. If Darwin's grandfather Erasmus Darwin and other Darwin family members already knew, accepted, believed, and taught a theory of evolution, then how could Charles have discovered it by some random chance?

Him: I still don't know about that.

Me: Feel free to research it. Here are some additional fun facts to ponder. First, there was a man named Alfred Wallace. You've probably never heard of him and have to wonder why he's not often mentioned. Perhaps it's because Wallace was a Catholic who had far more scientific credentials than Darwin. He believed that God had a hand in the evolutionary process. Or, perhaps he's not mentioned as often because much of his work may have been destroyed on his ship that went down in flames.

Wallace greatly contributed to the field and study of evolution. He and Charles Darwin used to correspond with each other and help each other to advance their findings. However, Wallace held that there could not be any purely naturalistic, materialist, or godless explanation of evolution. In other words, God was needed.

Furthermore, naturalistic accounts (i.e. how life came about without God) were presented long before even the Darwins. For example, a man named Epicurus who was a proponent of this belief had already taught and wrote on the subject more than 2000 years earlier.[18]

Him: Hmmm, still not convinced. I'm not so sure.

Me: Well, feel free to look it up for yourself. Research Erasmus Darwin. In any case, I think we can at least agree on the fact that science cannot explain life's origins.

Him: But we will someday. Science will figure out everything eventually.

Me: How do you know that? Can you prove that statement to me scientifically? If not, science cannot prove everything. [He pauses a while to think about it.]

[At this point, we were both feeling tired from our discussion that had gone on for at least two hours.]

---

[18] This section of information came from a book by Benjamin Wiker called, *The Darwin Myth*.

Me: [Tired of talking for two hours] Well, I don't know about you, but I have thoroughly enjoyed this conversation today. I like how we can just discuss things openly and honestly, and I hope we get to do it again sometime.

Him: Yeah, that would be nice. I enjoyed it too.

# CHAPTER 10

✧

# The Catholic Church
# And Sexual Abuse

## A Discussion about the Sex Abuse Scandal

---

*Setting:  A group of people were talking when one of them took God's name in vain.  I do not usually say anything, but today I decided to.*

Person #1:  Jesus Chr*st!

Me: [Casually] I love Jesus; please don't take His name in vain.

Person #2:  Oh, you are Catholic right?

Me: Yep!

Him: Oh! Well then, I have a question to ask you.  So, the

Church doesn't want gay people to marry but they are totally OK with priests molesting kids. How does that work? How is *that* OK?

Me: Umm... it's *not* OK.

Him: Then why does the Church allow it? I even think the pope helped to cover it up or endorse it or something.

[Observing that this was all just a conspiracy theory based on hearsay, I decided to help inform him.]

Me: OK, first of all, the pope endorsed nothing and covered up nothing. In actuality, it's a fact that Pope Benedict was one of the main whistle blowers on the sex abuse scandals, even when others wanted to him to keep quiet about it. The Pope also replaced 2-3 bishops a month removing corrupt ones and replacing them with better holy ones. He also...

[Interrupted by person #2]

Person #2: Then why is there such a huge problem? Look at all your priests who did stuff to kids!

Me: It's actually *not* a huge problem, and most priests by far are innocent. Allow me to back up for a moment and give you the facts. 85% of all sexual abuse takes place in the family. Nearly 15% of all cases happen in the *public schools*. [Interrupted again.]

Person #3: [Blurts out] How do you even know all this?

Me: [Ignoring him and continuing my train of thought] 15% takes place in the public schools. That's *100 times* more sexual abuse than in all religious institutions. Then, less than 1% of all sexual abuse happens in religious institutions, the least of which is the Catholic Church.

Student #2: Oh.

Me: Moreover, almost every single case you hear about over and over again on the news happened between 30-50 years ago! Almost all of the perpetrators are either dead, were "fired" (not the technical term), or are in jail.

Person #2: Oh, I didn't know that.

Me: Right, so the media is being dishonest and merely rehashing old stories most times. [Going back to person #3's question] The reason I know this is because I have studied it at length! Check out *John Jay College of Criminal Justice* and *Dr. Phillip Jenkins* who is not a Catholic. These are the foremost authorities on this issue. John Jay has done all the studies and has many statistics. Dr. Phillip Jenkins has studied it for decades. Check them out for yourself, and you will see that they confirm everything I am saying.

*End Note:* Everyone seemed satisfied with the answer, and nobody else had anything to say.

*Apologetics Note:* In evangelization, one of our main tasks is to clear up misconceptions that people have. As long as they have these misconceptions, they will view the Church and religion suspiciously. Clearing away objections they have is the first step toward bringing them back to God, the Church, and to the truth in general.

Also, the Catholic Church has taken many steps to ensure child safety and to make certain that nothing like this ever happens again. Dioceses all across America and even in other countries have instituted mandatory programs. (*Protecting God's Children* and *Child Lures* are two of those programs, just to name a couple).

Everyone working with children or teens is required to attend this mandatory course on how to recognize and prevent child sexual abuse. I've had to take it five times so far. For me, it seems unnecessarily overkill, but the Church is serious about this. The Catholic Church has taken numerous concrete measures which have not been taken in the public schools or anywhere else. That is important to know. The Catholic Church is now the safest institution in the country.

So, when people are outraged at the Church for sexual abuse, ask them why they are not also outraged at the public schools. Yes, the Church is more accountable since they claim a higher moral code, but if people are truly concerned about ending sexual abuse, they will stop being hypocritical and work to end it wherever it is, especially where it's the worst: families and schools. The Church has taken steps; why haven't they? Out of 44,000 priests in the USA, there have been only 6-7 credible accusations each year over the last 5 years or so. That's far less than 1%

✚

# CHAPTER 11

# The Bible Is Full Of Hate

## *Discussing the Bible and Morality*

---

*Introductory Note on Morality: There are people who believe morals are relative meaning that nothing is really right or wrong. In other words, there is no objective moral truth, and morality is different for each person. "What's true for you might not be true for me," and "Whatever you believe is acceptable as long as you don't hurt anyone else."*

*However, Christianity believes that there is an objective moral truth meaning that some things are right and wrong regardless of a person's personal opinion. For example, Hitler executed millions of innocent people in a horrific way. That was wrong. That's not an opinion; it's a fact. Moral relativism would not condemn Hitler for his actions though. According to that worldview, there is no such thing as an objectively evil action. They might personally disagree with what Hitler did but would ultimately have to respect his decision because it was Hitler's own personal belief. After all, "What's right for Hitler might not be right for them," they would say. Obviously, one can see how problematic and inhumane this flawed logic is.*

<u>*Setting*</u>*: One day, I had the pleasure of speaking with a teenage girl who had recently made her Confirmation.*

Her: I saw you talking with someone about God the other day. How did your conversation go?

Me: It went great! We talked for like an hour, and she really enjoyed it.

Her: I had a conversation with my dad the other day about religion too.

Me: Regarding what?

Her: We argued about Creationism. I don't agree with it.

Me: Me neither.

Her: Well, I just hate the whole Bible. The whole Bible is just false and stupid.

Me: You hate the *whole* Bible? Please tell me why.

Her: Because it just preaches hate. The whole thing is just hateful. I prefer the Satanic Bible.

There's a lot about love in there, and that book makes much more sense than the Bible.

Me: You're kidding, right?

Her: No, it has much better stuff in it than the Bible does.

Me: Oh really! Like the requirement to have as much anonymous sex with as many people you can? The requirement states that you're not even supposed to learn their names if at all possible. Yeah, that's *great* advice!

[There was another boy present who was listening to our conversation. My statement made him burst out loud laughing which simultaneously caused the girl to blush and attempt to justify her position.]

Her: Well, the Satanic Bible teaches love.

Me: Anonymous sex with many people is not love, and that is just one example. Besides, the Bible teaches love too. What about Jesus and all the loving things He said, taught, and did?

Her: Yeah, I like Jesus. He was loving. I don't have a problem with Jesus.

Me: Sooo, you don't hate the *whole* Bible.

Her: No, not the whole Bible.

Me: But you said you hated the whole Bible. [The boy laughs out loud again seeing that she was caught in another contradiction. He was clearly getting a kick out of our conversation.]

Her: I just don't like the Old Testament.

Me: So, you don't hate the *whole* Bible?[19]

Her: No, I just hate the whole Old Testament. Jesus is fine.

Me: Why do you hate the Old Testament?

Her: Because it preaches hate. All hate. Nothing but hate. Gays can't get together or anything.[20]

Me: What if *God* was the one who invented marriage and wanted it between a man and a woman?

Her: The Bible doesn't mention marriage. It just says don't sleep with each other.

---

[19] She originally said that she hated the whole Bible. I have now been able to make her admit that it's not all bad – a step in the right direction. I'm also holding her to her contradictions in a nice way, not moving too quickly onto another topic, but rather helping her to critically think out what she actually believes and why. This is necessary if people are going to see, recognize, and change their irrational beliefs.

[20] Aha! Now I see what the real root issue here is: it's a moral issue. Getting past people's smokescreens to the root cause of their problem is necessary for successful evangelization and for addressing the real issue.

Me: Actually, Adam and Eve were created by God as the first married couple who were brought together by Him. God Himself instructed them how to live. Jesus confirmed this in the New Testament.

Her: Well, if that's true, then I'm OK with that. But not sleeping with each other? I don't agree that you have to wait until marriage to sleep with someone. People should just be able to screw each other. After all, that would make happier marriages.

Me: Really? [My eyes widen at her blunt assertion.]

Her: Yes! I mean, would you want to marry someone you haven't slept with? I wouldn't. How do you know if they are good for you or not? How do you know if you're both compatible?

Me: Sooo, basically what you're telling me is that a person is like a car. You need to test drive them in order to see if they are compatible, to see if they are the right one to buy. If not, you return them as you would an inanimate object that you don't like or which doesn't fit your needs.

Boy: [The boy laughs out loud again] Oh man! That's an awesome analogy; there's *nothing* you can say to that.

Her: But...

Me: And think about this: 99% of marriage is *non-sexual*, *even* if you have sex a lot! That's important to know! This means that almost everything you do in marriage is *not* sexual. Therefore, it's *all the other things* in marriage and in life that are far more important. *These* are the things that make or break a marriage and make it truly happy.

Sex itself is great – and by the way, Catholics believe it's super awesome – but sexual compatibility is at the bottom of the list in terms of important items to consider when choosing a marriage partner. Things like good communication, friendship, virtue, common values, respect, and many other things are far more important and are what we should base our marital decisions on.

Her: [Sarcastically] Ohhh, so priests can molest kids, but other people can't sleep with each other?

Me: Ummm…

Her: I have a band I'm listening to, and they talk a lot about priests molesting kids.

Me: That means they might have been molested too, which is why they are so angry and why they talk about it so frequently. Here's a question for you: Does this band also talk about public school teachers molesting kids and what a horrible thing it is?

Her: [Completely caught off-guard] What??

Me: The sexual abuse of kids is *100 times* more prevalent in public schools than it is in religious organizations. Why don't they call out teachers and schools systems too?

Boy: Wow! I didn't know that.

Me: Yes, 85% of sexual abuse happens in the family. Nearly 15% happens in public school systems, and less than 1% happens in religious institutions of which the least is now the Catholic Church.

Boy: Wow, you know a lot on the statistics.

Me: Yes, I have studied this topic a lot.

Her: Good point. (She pauses to think about it silently. I give her time). But still, people should be able to do what they want. It's none of God's business what they do. I don't want to get married and have kids someday. I hate kids and don't want to deal with the likes of them.

Me: That's too bad. It sounds like you yourself have had a bad experience growing up as a kid.

Her: Yeah... I was adopted. And where I'm from, they kick you out of the country at a certain age if you're an orphan – or something like that.

Me: Aha, that makes sense now! So, you don't feel like you personally received love growing up and now can't imagine having children yourself.

Her: Yeah.

Me: Have you ever thought about having children and raising them better than your parents raised you, or your guardians raised you?

Her: No. Not really. I just don't want kids.

*End Note:* I left the conversation there. Making some headway and planting some seeds, I was happy with the conversation. Her issues were far too deep to penetrate in the short time we had. There were deep moral issues and personal issues that would need to be probed. My inner voice told me to stop and just pray for her. Maybe someday as she grows, heals, and matures, she will think differently and remember some of the things that we spoke about.

✟

# CHAPTER 12

# The Search For God

## *A Conversation with an Open Agnostic*

---

*Side Note:* *This is a long and in-depth conversation which offers deeper scientific and philosophical arguments for God. If you find it over your head, I would recommend trying to persevere through it. You may find it helpful to re-read the difficult parts over again until they begin to make sense. It also addresses the question of why God allows suffering.*

*Setting:* *I received a phone call from an atheist across the country who had many questions about God. An acquaintance had recommended that he speak to me. He was sincere but passionate. Every time he asked me a question, he would cut me off before I could even respond, and he would give me a long list of objections that he had against the existence of God. After a few times of not being allowed to speak, it occurred to me that this man just needed to vent and had a lot to get off his chest. So, I let him. After a while of letting it all out, he allowed me to start answering his questions which is where this conversation begins. For this reason, I have not included everything he said but a summary of his main objections.*

Atheist: So, I'm just wondering why you believe in God? What I mean by that is, do you have any evidence for God's existence? It just seems obvious to me that God does not exist. Moreover, it doesn't seem that there is any good evidence to support the claim of God.

Me: That's a good objection, and I would be happy to talk to you about this today. I'm really glad you called, and I hope to be able to help a bit. Where should we start?

Him: How could there be a God? And why does there *have* to be a God? Doesn't evolution answer the question of where we came from in terms of the beginning of life? And, doesn't the Big Bang give sufficient evidence for where we came from in general? Don't you think it's better to go with science rather than faith?

Me: So, basically you would like to know why I believe in God and what evidence there is. Sure, I would be happy to share that with you... First, from a very subjective point of view, I believe in God because He changed my life. I used to be a teenager who dressed in all black, carried weapons, and was angry at the world. I had no self-esteem and lived in with depression, loneliness, and sadness for many years. God was the one who pulled me out of that mess, set me on solid ground, and gave me new life, along with great peace, light, joy, love, and freedom! So, I don't believe in God because I learned about Him from some book or because of some religious education classes. Rather, I believe in God because He changed my life and made me incredibly happy.

As to the more logical reasons, there are several of which I will only name a few. First, there is the argument that *something cannot come from nothing*. And, our experience of science confirms this. For instance, if you take the number zero (which represents nothing) and add another zero to it, you would still have zero. $0 + 0$ is always 0. 100 trillion, trillion, trillion zeros plus zero is still zero. You can add as many zeros as you would like and the outcome is always the same. Zero. It's the same with nothing.

If there was absolutely nothing in the beginning, then there would be absolutely nothing still now because something cannot come from nothing. The fact that we have something in existence at all shows that there *had* to be someone or something who already possessed existence in the first place.

For example, take a group of 50 people in a small room who all have to read the exact same book. If none of the people actually have a copy of the book, then nobody can read it or give it to anyone else. In other words, *you can't give what you yourself don't have!*[21] Likewise, if there was nothing in existence (nothing there, no-existence) then there would be nothing that had existence of its own and therefore could not

---

[21] The book analogy came from: *The Handbook of Catholic Apologetics,* by Peter Kreeft and Ronald Tacelli.

give it away to anything else (exactly like all the people in the room who didn't possess a book and therefore couldn't give it away).

Nothing makes nothing. Nothing does nothing. Nothing is nothing. Something (existence) can't come from nothing (non-existence). It's doesn't make sense. It's impossible. Nothing cannot give what it doesn't have... existence.

If there was only nothing, then there would only be nothing forever. Therefore, there absolutely had to be Someone who did possess existence by His very nature and who could then give existence, share that existence, with everything else. Christians call that being God. *God is existence itself.* He doesn't *have* existence, He *is* existence. Because of this, He can share that existence and give it to other things, which makes Him the absolute Creator.

Him: Yeah, but how do you know it's God? How do we know it's not the universe? How do we know it's not something else?

Me: God is the name that we give to the Supreme Being. It's a generic term for the One who created all things. Yet, your point brings us to another argument, the Kalam argument. The Kalam argument states:

1. Everything that comes into existence (or begins to exist) has a cause
2. The universe began to exist
3. Therefore, the universe must have a cause

This is an argument that has been used for nearly a thousand years, and no one has been able to refute it effectively. It demonstrates that the universe cannot cause itself or be its own cause. Rather, there is a cause and effect, and the effect cannot be the cause. The cause has to transcend the universe and all created things.

Him: OK, I get that. [Thinking silently about it] But, you said everything has a cause. So, who caused God? Where did He come from? Who made Him?

Me: I did not say that *everything* has a cause, but everything that *begins to exist* has a cause. God did not begin to exist and so does not have a cause. Asking who made God is like asking why a triangle has four sides. The question doesn't make sense because by definition a triangle has three sides, and by definition, God is eternal, uncreated, and didn't come into existence. God has no beginning and no end.

If God *was* made, He wouldn't be anything more special than you or me who were made, or the stars, or the trees, or anything else in creation. Yet, God infinitely surpasses His creation and transcends it. Think about this. If God was made... then He would not be God! Whatever created Him probably would be. Who could create God anyway? It doesn't make sense. By definition, God is the eternal Creator who creates everything else and not the one who is created.

Now, some people have a hard time imagining or understanding this. And, that is good. If we could fully comprehend God, He would be pretty lame. After all, there are so many things in this universe that we can't even understand. God is infinitely beyond all universes, and so to think that we could ever understand God completely is fallacious. It's not going to happen.

However, just because something is difficult to understand doesn't mean it's not true. I don't understand calculus and find it confusing, but that doesn't mean it's not true. Rather, all deep things like mathematics were true long before people came to understand it. It's the same with God. He is true and real even if we can't fully comprehend Him right now.

Him: OK, that makes some sense.

Me: Great! Then, following up from where I left off... whatever created the universe cannot be part of the universe but must be beyond it. The Big Bang itself shows us that matter, time, space, and energy all came *into* existence (received existence) at one singular point, before which presumably, they did not exist.

God is eternal, and since matter came into existence and had a beginning, then whatever created the universe cannot be made of matter, thus making this being immaterial (spiritual, if you will). Also, since space and time came into existence at the Big Bang, the Creator must also be outside of space and time making this being spaceless and eternal. You can start to see a clearer picture of God developing and coming into focus once we understand these things. Obviously, this being must be extremely powerful and intelligent too.

This brings us to our next arguments for God's existence: contingency and efficient causality. This is similar to what was stated before. Basically, *nothing can create itself.* Also, no created thing has the power to *keep itself in existence.* Everything comes into and goes out of existence, and we have no power over that. This is because everything in the universe is contingent (dependent) on something else for its existence, or rather, on many other things.

I will give an example of this starting with myself. I did not (nor could I) create myself. Also, I cannot keep myself in existence, and I will certainly die someday no matter how healthy or strong I become. Moreover, I am dependent on other things for my life.

For instance, I came from my parents, who came from their parents, who came from their parents, and so on down the line. We are all dependent. Moreover, I am dependent on food, oxygen, gravity, nurturing, and much more in order to live. Every created thing is contingent (has this dependency) in this way. Everything.

Even if you go back to the early parts of the universe, every single thing still depends on other things, or rather, many other things for their existence. For example, carbon and oxygen come from stars. Stars come from helium, hydrogen and other gases. Hydrogen and helium come from other things, and so on.

In other words, if stars did not exist, carbon and oxygen would not either. If helium and hydrogen did not exist, neither would stars, carbon, oxygen, or anything else that all stem from that chain. You get the point. Since every created thing is contingent and dependent on something else, not one of these things can be the creator of itself or the sole cause of anything else. It's like following a line of dominoes all the way back to the first domino. Someone had to push that first domino and get the whole chain reaction started.

Another example, look at a man pushing a round rock down the street with a stick. The stick cannot move itself. The rock cannot move itself. Only the human body is capable of moving on its own, but even then, humans share in a line of contingency. The hand which is holding the stick is dependent on the wrist, which relies on the arm, which depends on the shoulder, and so on. Humans also rely on food, oxygen, gravity, and many other things. All of these must be present for humans to live, breath, move, and to go about freely.

Moreover, all of these things are in turn dependent on other things, and they all need to exist at once *simultaneously*, for everything else to exist and stay in existence. Consequently, none of these created things are God. They did not create themselves, nor are they able to keep themselves in existence. Rather, they are all dependent on a higher power, a transcendent Power who in turn is *not dependent* on anyone or anything for its existence.

Another way to get at this is by looking at the difference between actuality and potentiality. Some things are *actually* moving and are actually in motion (actuality). Other things, for whatever reason cannot move at all and have *no power* to move on their own. However, they have the *potential* to move (potentiality). Dead, inanimate objects are potential because they have *no power to actually move themselves* (to actualize themselves). Rather, they *require someone or something else* to set them into motion (This is why the universe cannot be God and cannot be eternal. Elements, matter, forces, and the like are all potential and have no actuality (no power to move or do anything of themselves)!

Take a book for example. A book sitting on a dinner table requires someone or something else to move it, right? It has no power to actualize itself or to set itself into motion, right? However, it *becomes actual* (it actually moves) when someone else moves it. Like the book, *no dead thing can actualize itself or put itself into motion.* They are purely potential (meaning they only have the potential to move *if something else* moves it). We can start to see why God who is a being of pure actuality is needed to bring every created thing (all potential in some way) into existence.

Living creatures like humans and animals are *part* actuality with *some* power to actualize themselves or other things. I say *part* actuality because not even human beings are pure actuality. Rather, we depend on other things too to exist, to live, and to move, as we spoke about earlier (food, gravity, oxygen, etc.). Even though we are partly potential (meaning we are dependent on other things), we are also partially actual (meaning that we do have the ability and power to move ourselves, to think, act, and create, etc.).

This is the important point. God is the only being that is *pure actuality*, and He has to be! Since dead things do not have any power to move or actualize anything – including themselves – there could not have been just *nothing* in the beginning.

If God did not exist, there would be nothing. And, nothing has no power to actualize anything or to bring anything into existence. This can only happen through the power of pure actuality. Things that were brought into existence are purely potential (meaning they have only the potential to exist). They had to be *actualized* or set into motion by some outside source that has the power to do so.

The created universe is purely potential and so could not be the cause of itself. That is like saying a dead book could create itself out of nothing and then create more books. No. Books need to be created and *brought into being* by something that already has being and the power to do so. Only a being of pure actuality (pure act and power) can create the universe from nothing, or anything from nothing. This is also why the universe cannot be eternal.

It's one purely potential thing depending on another purely potential thing depending on another purely potential thing, which must inevitably arrive at a first Cause who has the power to put it all into motion – to move it from potentially moving to actually moving. Otherwise, if there is only a line of potential things, this eventually leads to contradiction since a potential line cannot go back forever without coming to something that can actualize it or start it all in the first place. Only God is dependent on nothing and relies on no one. He is pure actuality Who is the cause of everything else. He is perfect, infinite, unchanging.

Only someone that actually exists can bring other things into existence. "Nothing" doesn't have the power to do that. For example, humans already exist and so have the power to create and bring other things into existence (buildings, computers, civilizations, etc.).

It's the same with God. Everything in existence that we observe could not exist if there was not Someone *already in existence* to call it forth. Therefore, there has to be a Being of pure actuality who is existence itself and who has the power to bring everything into existence. What do you think about that?

Him: Wow! That's really deep. I'm not sure I could follow all of it, but some of it made sense. [Silence. Afterward, his tone of voice is much more sincere and even curious.] Can I ask you another question? There are so many religions out there, which one is right? They all claim to be right and yet they all believe different things. So, doesn't that tell you religion was just made up, perhaps?

Me: No, not really. Just because there are different versions of history regarding the Civil War does not mean that they are *all* wrong or that the Civil War never took place. Just because there are different religions, doesn't mean that God is not real or that one religion is not correct.

The way I look at it is this. There is something in the heart of all men across the globe, a hunger for their Creator, a hunger for the truth, and a hunger for deeper meaning, something animals don't have. Man seeks God innately. It's important to realize that most, if not all, of the major world religions share many of the same core beliefs.

Additionally, I would also argue that most of mankind believes in the one same all-powerful Creator being, though they may have different understandings of who He is. For example, imagine a TV channel that people around the world are watching at the same time. Some people are watching it on a 70-inch HDTV (high definition television) while others a 21-inch poor quality TV, and still others on a 13-inch television with bad reception and a fuzzy picture, etc.

So, they are all watching the same channel, but not everyone has a clear picture or a full understanding of what they are looking at. Perhaps we all seek God so much because deep inside us, He has placed that desire within our hearts.

Him: All religions claim that their religion is the only true one, and all others are going to hell. How can you all think you're the right one and just condemn everyone else who disagrees with you?

Me: I can only speak as a Catholic, but Catholics don't condemn anybody. While we absolutely believe that the Catholic Church has the fullness of truth and that Jesus is the only way to heaven, this does not mean that we condemn all other religions. The Church teaches that only God can be the final judge. We can sometimes judge actions, but we can never judge a person's heart or where they will go for eternity.

Him: That's good to hear. But what if somebody doesn't believe in Jesus?

Me: The Catholic Church teaches that Jesus is *necessary* for salvation, and that everyone who is saved (whether they realize it or not) will be saved through Jesus Christ. So, the closer someone is to Jesus and what He taught, the easier it will be for them to attain eternal life.

With that being said, let's say there's a Buddhist in the remote mountains of China who dies and arrives at Judgment Day; God's not going to say, "Go to hell." The Buddhist would reply, "Why Lord?" The answer: "Because you didn't believe in my Son Jesus." "But sir, I have never even heard the name of Jesus in my life." "Aww, that's tough luck," God retorts, "but you're going to hell anyway. Ciao."

No, God is not unjust, and this is not the kind of God that Catholics believe in. In fact, the Bible teaches that God is perfectly just, and therefore, God would not send somebody to hell unjustly. What the Catholic Church teaches is that if somebody did not know Jesus and His truth, and it was *by no fault of their own* (meaning there was absolutely no way they could have known the truth), then it's possible for them to be saved.

God will judge them according to what they knew and how

they lived their lives. Some people live the truth of Jesus without even knowing Him. One thing is clear; no one who has an evil heart or who intentionally rejects God and His truth will enter into heaven.

Him: That makes sense. Do you want to know what my big problem with the whole religion thing is? It's this.[22] There is *so much* suffering on this earth. How do you explain that? If God is so powerful, He could stop suffering. If God is love, He would *want* to stop all the suffering wouldn't He? Yet, there is suffering.

So, either God is not all-powerful or He is not all-loving. Or, He just doesn't exist. I mean, why would a good and loving God permit all the suffering on this earth? Innocent babies are dying! If you saw an innocent child being murdered, wouldn't you do something about it? If you saw someone being abused, wouldn't you try to stop it?

Me: Definitely! Of course I would. But, before I answer that, allow me to back up to the first part of your question. God is certainly powerful enough to stop suffering, and He will do so someday at the end of time. But, to say that God is not loving because He doesn't stop all suffering is not quite accurate. There are different ways to look at this.

Remember that Adam and Eve once had no suffering at all. Then, they rebelled against God and chose His enemy when they ate from the fruit of the forbidden tree. They tried to

---

[22] Aha! Here comes the root cause for his atheism.

become God without God. *They* brought suffering and death into the world at that point. They pushed God and His perfection away. With that being said, I do believe that there are many possible reasons that He *allows* suffering.

First, it teaches us compassion and love for others as we help those in need. That's a good thing, perhaps a much greater good than allowing us to become selfish and self-centered. Also, it reminds us of how little we are and how completely dependent on God we are rather than falling into the same pride Adam and Eve had when they first disobeyed God.

It also reminds us that this world is not eternal but is passing away. Heaven is our ultimate destination and has no pain or suffering. Perhaps the greatest reason though why there is suffering is because God has given us freewill. In order for Him to remove all suffering, He would also have to remove all free will and make us into robots.

Him: Yeah, but wouldn't that be better?

Me: I hardly think so. Imagine that scenario for a moment. Imagine no free will. It's kind of like playing a game of chess. Every time you are about to capture one of your opponent's pieces, he reaches over and takes *your piece* off the board before you play.[23] Now it's true that none of his pieces will get hurt or lose their life, but one cannot play a game that way either.

---

[23] Example taken from C.S. Lewis's work: *The Problem of Pain*.

It's the same in real life. God could make us numb, obedient robots. We might not have pain, but imagine not being able to choose your favorite food, enjoy the sun, the outdoors, family, or life at all. Imagine not having the capability to choose friends or have romantic relationships because you are not capable of choosing love. I don't think anyone would want to go without these things.

Here is something else to think about. What is *good*? Take a sports player who complains about how the coach works his players to the bone every day for three straight hours. He whines incessantly about it to everyone.

Now imagine a player who *loves* the three hour practices because he enjoys being on a championship team and winning. He knows that he has worked hard to become an all-state player and enjoys bettering himself. Here you have two players on the exact same team but with completely different attitudes. One views the practices as needless pain and suffering while the other sees the suffering as a good, something that makes him better.

The spectrum of good is possibly infinite. For example, imagine a person who steals, murders, and abuses others. Now imagine a second person who steals but who would never murder. Would not this second person seem "good" in comparison? A third person who doesn't murder or steal would seem even higher up on the good scale compared to the other two. And what about different levels of kindness and those like Mother Theresa who excel in virtue, sacrifice, and compassion?

God is the ultimate good and sees things in a way we cannot. God can even bring a greater good out of a really bad situation if He chooses. Remember that *the greatest good in God's eyes is to get us to heaven.* He will even allow some physical suffering in our lives if it helps us to turn back to Him, save our souls, and arrive at our final destination of heaven.

C.S. Lewis once said that suffering is the megaphone of God yelling out to us and trying to get our attention. With that being said, God doesn't want us to suffer alone. Therefore, He Himself came to earth in the person of Jesus Christ. He entered into our suffering and had a share in it. The culmination of this was His crucifixion on the cross. With that act, He would take and redeem suffering once and for all. His resurrection is also a foreshadowing of ours.

For this reason, even in the darkest and most difficult circumstances of our lives, we can still find peace and joy in Jesus Christ who is our strength. This deep peace can *only* be found in Jesus by giving our lives to Him. He is the answer our hearts are looking for!

Now, let me ask you a question. Really think deeply about this! What if you could take a pill that would kill all the pain in your life? You will not suffer anymore or feel anything for the rest of your days. The side effect though is that this drug would put you into a complete vegetative state. You can't move, think, or do anything but sit in a corner for the rest of your life with no ability to choose or to live. But you are pain free. Which would you choose?[24]

Him: Hmmm. *Wow*! That's a *really* good question. I see your point. [He thinks about it silently for a while.] Yeah, I understand what you're saying. That makes sense. One thing that just makes me angry though is innocent children who are abused or babies dying for no reason. Let's say you had a son and somebody comes in and kills him cold blood. Wouldn't you be angry?

Me: Absolutely! That would be horrific and heartbreaking. However, it would be far more sad for an atheist like yourself. Atheists believe that life ends after death and that there is nothing else. End of story. So, when an innocent child dies, it's a huge tragedy, but there's nothing that can be done.

However, from a Christian perspective, death is not the end. That child will go straight to heaven where they will never experience pain or suffering again for all eternity. In heaven, they will be completely happy and fulfilled. So, while it is a huge tragedy here on earth, death is not the end but only the beginning.

In reality, it would be better for the innocent child in heaven because they will never have to experience the horrible abuses and tragedies this life dishes out. And remember, God is a God of justice. The killer or abuser will receive a

---

[24] This example comes from the book, *Catholic Realism: Framework for the Refutation of Atheism and the Evangelization of Atheists*.

just judgment and will not get away with his atrocities. We have that promise as Christians. But where is the justice in the atheistic view? There is none. Something awful happens, and that's it. There's nothing that can be done except grieve and move on.

I feel the Christian view is far better and far more just. In the Christian worldview, there is hope, and there is a much better life awaiting those who have their lives taken unfairly. And make no mistake, it *is* unfair. But the Christian view offers recompense where the atheistic alternative does not. Does that make sense in some way?

Him: Yes, actually it does... a lot!

*End Note:* Our conversation ended here. The atheist pondered everything silently for a short while. Then, he graciously thanked me for the conversation and informed me that I had given him a lot to think about. Naturally, I prayed for this man and his search. Perhaps he will someday return to the God who created him, gave him life, and who loves him with an infinite love.

# CHAPTER 13

✧

# Does God Love *Me*?

## *Discussions on Abortion and Homosexuality*

---

*Setting: Many years ago, I taught at an alternative high school for troubled teens. One day, a group of them were all huddled around a computer in the corner. They called me over to look at some gory shark attack pictures complete with swimmers missing limbs. They say nothing can shock teenagers nowadays, but I discovered that is not always the case.*

Girl: Yo Mista (short for Mr. Mercier), come check this out.

Me: What are you looking at here?

Girl: Shark attacks. Yo, that's gross, right?

Me: Yeah, that's pretty gross.

Boy: Pretty gross? That's nasty son!

Me: [Just speaking honestly off the top of my head] It's not as bad as some other things that I've seen.

Girl: Yeah right Mista. What you seen that's worse than this?

Me: Pictures of abortion.

Boy: Yeah right. You buggin.

Girl: I'm gonna check it out right now, for real yo. [She goes to Google images and looks up abortion pictures. Not exactly what I foresaw would happen.]

Girl: [Her mouth drops] YO! No waaayyy. Check that out!! [Covers her mouth in shock] Yo, that's messed up!

Boy: Mista, is that for real?

Me: Yes, that's for real.

Girl: Yo, that is messed up! I ain't never gonna have any abortion. No way!

~      ~      ~

*Setting: I was walking down a street in Boston when a young lady called out to me.*

Her: Excuse me sir, could you please help us save animals?

Me: What do you mean? What are you trying to do?

Her: A lot of people abuse and even kill animals, and so we are trying to stop the abuse and save them.

Me: [After a moment of thought] Can I ask you a seemingly random question first?

Her: Sure.

Me: Are you pro-life or pro-choice?

Her: [Instantly confused as to what that had to do with anything] Ummm…. well… I'm personally pro-life, but I also don't think we should tell women what to do with their own bodies.

Me: Hmm. [I think about it for a moment and then politely respond.] Well, to me, *all* human life is incredibly precious, so when you start working to save the lives of human beings who are being abused and killed in abortion, I will help you to save the lives of animals that are being abused.

[The young lady's mouth literally dropped as she stood there dumfounded thinking over the comment. She had nothing to say after that. I just smiled and wished her a great day.]

*End Note:* A better way to have phrased the last statement would have been to use her own logic against her in the same manner saying: "Well, I am *personally* pro-animal and not for abusing or killing them, but I also don't think that we should tell owners what to do with their own animals inside the privacy of their own homes. It's their choice after all."

This would have been like an atomic bomb, and the irony would have been deafening. Does anyone really think that we should let people do what they want to their own animals? No. Likewise, can we really accept that human beings should have the choice to kill their own babies in the womb? The answer is also no.

*Apologetics Note:* Here are a few reasons of many that a woman cannot choose abortion.

1. The baby is not just "her body." The child is its *own* individual life *distinct* from the mother and complete with its own set of DNA. In other words, it's not just removing a lump from the body; it's taking an actual human life.

2. Also, it is not the case that the mother's body is just "her body." Our bodies and our whole lives are a gift from God, and this gift comes with great responsibility. We will have to answer to the Lord for what we have done and for how we have treated our bodies in this life that He has given us.

3. Choosing to take an innocent life is never acceptable for any reason. The baby is the most innocent and helpless person on earth; we must work to protect their lives and not

destroy them. Some people attempt to say that they aren't persons. However, every time we try to take someone's personhood away bad things happen. Just look at Hitler and the Jews, for example. Hitler said the Jews weren't persons and look what the result was.

The same could be said for slavery in the United States. Also, there are some people in our government today that don't think people become persons until 7 years old, until the age of reason. I have heard others say 3 years old. The point is, once you take away personhood, atrocities follow.

The truth is that the innocent child within the womb has a heartbeat, brain waves, and can feel pain. It just needs time and food. It is a very small person but a person nonetheless.

Mother Teresa once said; "I feel that the greatest destroyer of peace today is abortion because it is a war against the child, a direct killing of the innocent child. And if we accept that a mother can kill even her own child, how can we tell other people not to kill one another?"

~     ~     ~

*Setting:* *Another conversation with an inner city teen.*

Girl: Yo Mista. You're religious right?

Me: Yes, I'm religious. [Smile]

Her:  Will you pray to God for me?

Me:  Sure!  But why don't you pray for yourself?

Her:  Cause God don't like me.

Me:  What?  Why not?  Why wouldn't God like you?

Her:  [Silent for a second] Cause I'm gay.

[I'm not sure why, but I became instantly angry at that point. It was not at her, but rather, because this poor girl from the hood thought God hated her just because she was gay.  She was lied to.]

Me:  Who told you that?  Actually, it doesn't matter. Whoever told you that *lied* to you!  See, God made us all, and that means we are *all* His children no matter what our sexuality is.  You are His child and He loves you as much as He loves Mother Teresa or the Pope.

Her:  Really?  [She thinks about it deeply for a few seconds or so.] Cool, cool.  [Excited] I'm gonna go home and pray to God tonight.

Me:  Good for you!  That will put a big smile on God's face.

*End Note:* Everything I said in this conversation was true.  I never endorsed any behaviors, and there was no reason to talk about anything else since she didn't even know God or His love.  One thing alone was necessary, to let this girl know that she was loved by God unconditionally and to move her toward a relationship with Him.

~      ~      ~

*Setting: This is a typical conversation that I have had a few times with some different people:*

Boy #1:  Hey, look at the kid over there.  He is so gay.

Boy #2:  Yeah!  Sooo gay.

Me:  Really?  So what?

Boy #1:  Huh?

Boy #2:  Wait what? [confused] Are *you* gay?

Me:  Not at all.  I've been happily married for years.  I just do not think someone should be made fun of because they are different than you.

[Both boys say nothing.  They just look at each other, shrug their shoulders, and walk away.]

~      ~      ~

*Setting:* *I was substitute teaching for a high school English class and typing away fiercely on my laptop. As the students were handing in their work for the day, one girl lingered a little longer. She seemed to have something on her mind.*

Her: Hey, Mr. Mercier. You are a Catholic, right?

Me: Yes.

Her: [With a downcast voice] Oh. So, then do you hate... [She trails off, and for some reason, I knew exactly what she was thinking.]

Me: Gays?

Her: Yeah.

Me: No. Not at all! I try to love all people the same.

Her: But you're Catholic, aren't you? Doesn't the Catholic Church hate...

Me: Gays?

Her: Yeah.

Me: Some people in the Catholic Church do, but they are wrong to do so. The master we serve is Jesus Christ, and He taught us that we should love everyone equally. And, everyone means everyone! What's funny is that some people think I'm gay because I stick up for them all the time.

Her: [Her face instantly brightens up.] Wow! Ya know, I really like you Mr. Mercier. You are a great person!

Me: Thank you! [Big smile]

*Evangelization Note*: This is how all Christians should treat others – with respect and dignity – even people they may disagree with. We cannot possess an "us vs. them" attitude. While we might not agree with everything they stand for or some particular views or lifestyles they hold, we can still love a person as Jesus would have loved them.

Note that I never claimed to be for or against homosexuality because that wasn't the question. I didn't condone the action by not condemning it which many falsely think happens. You can love someone without agreeing with everything they do. The question was about hating others which we as Christians cannot do – ever.

Thus, that's the topic I focused on and stayed on. It was not necessary to go anywhere else. Moreover, love and respect are the indispensable foundations one must have if we ever hope to breach this subject successfully. That's the starting point.

~    ~    ~

*Setting: I was invited to debate the question of whether God exists with a small group of people – mostly atheists.*

*Toward the end, someone asked me some hot button questions on the subject of homosexuality.*

Girl #1: I would like to know your thoughts on the Bible and homosexuality. Specifically, what do you think about gay marriage? The book of Leviticus says that homosexuality is an abomination, but the book of Matthew, chapter 7, tells us not to judge. So what do you have to say about that?

Me: I will answer the second part first. Some parts of the Bible say that we can't judge people while other parts of the Bible say we *can* judge. The Bible does not contradict itself but is speaking about judging in different ways.

For example, Matthew 7 is telling us that we cannot judge a person's *heart* or intention. In addition, we cannot ever condemn anyone or say who is or who is not going to hell because we are not God. In other words, we cannot know the state of a person's heart or their eternal destination.

On the other hand, the Bible does state that we can and should judge certain *actions* that are wrong and sinful (1 Cor. 6:3-4; Mt. 18:15-18). For example, if somebody murders another person, would you say, "We can't judge." No, you would say, "That is wrong!" Let's take Hitler, for example, who murdered millions of people in horrific ways. We cannot sit back and say, "No judgment here. He's allowed to do what he wants, and we can't judge him."

Of course we can judge his deeds and even condemn his actions as evil. However, we could never judge Hitler's eternal salvation. That's God's job. He may have converted on his deathbed. We do not know. So, the Bible speaks of different kinds of judging. The judging condemned in Matthew 7 is falsely judging someone's heart or condemning their soul as if you were God. Does that answer your question?

Boy #1: You would make a great politician, ya know! You conveniently didn't answer her central question.

Me: Which question?

Him: What are your thoughts on gay marriage?

Me: Oh yes! Thank you for reminding me. The answer is that I'm *for* homosexuals, but I'm not for gay *marriage*. Before I even expound on that, you have to understand something important. Everyone needs to be fully aware that God loves all homosexuals – a lot! He loves them as much as Mother Teresa or even the pope himself. It's true! We are *all* God's children, and He desires a deep relationship with each and every one of us. With that being said, I'm not for homosexual marriage and here's why.

Marriage is between a man and a woman. That's the way it has always been forever. Nowadays, people are seeking to redefine marriage to include two persons of the same sex who "truly love each other." However, if we begin to change what marriage is in order to make it something else, then what's to stop us from allowing 3, 5, or even 10 people to marry who "truly love each other?"

This is known as polygamy (or polyamorous love), and there are hundreds of thousands of people in our country pushing hard to pass a law so that marriage can be redefined to include polygamy. This would allow a man to marry many women at the same time.

In addition, there are hundreds of thousands of people trying to legalize incest marriage (meaning a father can marry his son, or a sister can marry her brother, etc.). Now, we might remark how "messed up" that is, but these people will respond, "Why shouldn't two people of the same family who truly love each other not be able to get married? Why should we be discriminated against?"

Girl #2: Eww, that's...

Me: *Wait*! It gets worse. There are also many people in this country who are seeking to pass a law to make it legal for people to marry animals.

Girl #2: OK, that's gross!

Me: *We* believe that it's gross (and it is), but these people will respond by saying, "Who are you to tell me that I can't marry my animal if I truly love it? Who are you to tell me what I can and can't do in my own bedroom?" Can you see the rhetorical phrases people keep using in the same way to justify their actions?

However, none of it changes the bottom line that marriage has always been between a man and a woman forever.

That's what marriage *is*. Marriage is not whatever we want it to be. Therefore, I'm not for changing marriage *in any case*, whether it's homosexuality, polygamy, incest, animal marriage, or anything else. Once Pandora's Box is open everything can be permitted. So again, I'm not against homosexual *people*; they're great. However, I am against homosexual marriage *and any other type* of a relationship that would change what marriage really is.

Girl #3: That is fascinating. I have never thought about it in that way before. [Others agree.]

Me: Here's something else to consider. Imagine this. Imagine for a second that there were *only two women on earth*. That's it. No one else. Just two women. Or, imagine if God had only made *two men* instead of a man and a woman. What would happen?

[No answer]

Me: We would go extinct! If there were only two men or two women on earth, we would go extinct as a species because they cannot reproduce. So, all religion aside, a man and a woman each have the necessary body parts that fit together and work together perfectly in order to reproduce and keep life going on the planet. That's the way we were made just naturally speaking. This demonstrates that man and woman were meant to be together. Those are the big reasons, but there are others too.

Boy #2: Oh wow, that makes total sense!

Me: Another reason is complementarity. Man and woman are compatible for more reasons than just their body parts. They also complement each other emotionally and in other ways which are absolutely essential for marriage and for the good of children. What do I mean by that?

Well, it's no secret that men are not women and women are not men. Men act one way and offer certain qualities that women do not, and women act as women and offer feminine qualities in a way that men cannot. In other words, a man cannot replace a woman and vice-versa. Just as their bodies work together perfectly to produce life, so also their personalities, emotions, and masculine/feminine qualities work together to make a whole, healthy, and complete child.

That is why some children of homosexual parents have recently "come out" against homosexual marriage because they say from experience that a child needs both a mother and a father. One popular woman who grew up with two moms recently came out about this. She shared the disappointment of never having a father or a male figure in her life, something she needed.

She expressed a deep love for both of her mothers. And, even though her "mothers" did well raising her, they could never replace a father despite what some may say. As much as she loved them, she really needed a daddy too, something a mother (or two mothers) could never be.

Even if there are two dads, one more masculine and one more effeminate, they can never be or replace an actual woman. They are not made that way. Girls (and boys) need a dad. They also need a mother, and even the best father could never take the place of mommy. Men and women are different and offer different attributes and qualities that boys and girls each need. To have complete, whole children, a father and mother are both needed. That is complementarity, and that is the way we were made.

Another thing: marriage is more than just love.[25] Marriage is supposed to be a stable place for children to grow up in a wholesome environment where they can learn to be a moral and healthy part of society. With this being said, most people don't realize or understand how the homosexual lifestyle goes against this.

For example, it is very common for people of same-sex attraction [usually males] to have hundreds and even thousands of partners in a lifetime, *even* if they are married. This is incredibly rare in the heterosexual world. In fact, two homosexuals with a pro-gay agenda did an extensive study on monogamy among long-term gay couples. In the study, they sought to find couples who were completely monogamous with each other for more than five years. In the end, they could not find even one couple.[26]

---

[25] If it was *only* about love, what's wrong with incest? Or, why can't an old man marry a nine-year-old? After all, they love each other. Marriage is about far more than just two people "loving each other."

[26] Some people point out that there is divorce and unfaithfulness among heterosexuals too and that some children grow up in single family homes. This is true, but there is a monumental difference between the two. In homosexuality, there is *never* the possibility of a child growing up with a

Bryan Mercier

There may be one couple here or there, but these are extremely rare if they exist. Gay magazines often address the open relationships that same sex couples have with each other as something normal and expected. They continually offer advice on how to discuss this topic with your partner and how to successfully make it work.

I heard of another statistic which came out recently on homosexual men which revealed that almost 100% of them were infected with some kind of a disease.[27] Additionally, nearly 50% of them admitted to having 500-1000 sexual partners while another 27% admitted to having 1000 or more partners. Of course, this is not remotely healthy physically, psychologically, or emotionally, and it's not good for family life or for children.

---

man *and* a woman, a mom *and* a dad. Second, most children have had both of their parents for a good chunk of their life before the divorce happens. Thus, they have both parents for a while and can learn from them. Third, as stated above in the study, two gay men couldn't find any monogamy among homosexual long-term couples... not to mention their hundreds or thousands of partners in a life time. The parallel for this cannot be found among heterosexuals. Most heterosexuals are faithful, don't have hundreds or thousands of partners, and don't have the same drug addictions, diseases, early mortality rates, depression, suicidal tendencies, or other problems. This can be easily verified even from pro-gay websites.

[27] Gay websites and magazines continually write about many issues that homosexuals struggle with: high drug usage, eating disorders, suicide, rampant disease, and a short life expectancy, among others things. These are all catastrophically higher among homosexuals to a point that is shocking.

This was confirmed again by a study that one lady did from the University of Arizona. She did extensive research into male homosexuality and discovered that there is no fidelity among male homosexuals, not even long term couples. It's basically non-existent. She presented her findings to a board of eight members. Six out of the eight were homosexuals. The chairman of the board who himself was a homosexual called this lady into his office. To her surprise, he disclosed to her that her studies and findings were correct.[28]

He related that he and his partner were the "poster children" for homosexual couples but themselves were not faithful to each other. They had an open relationship. He candidly admitted that they *acted* faithful in public so they could get more acceptance in society, but in reality, they were not. Thus, even homosexuals admit to rampant infidelity even in long term couples. This is not good or healthy for marriage or for children.

One woman who grew up with a homosexual dad reveals how she accidentally walked in on her father having sex with several other men at the same time.[29] This traumatized her. One problem among many here is that our hearts were made for one partner and were not made for this kind of rampant sexual activity.

Lastly, there is one more thought that I have from a religious

---

[28] *Homosexuality, Why not?* by Janet Smith
[29] *Out From Under: The Impact of Homosexual Parenting,* by Dawn Stefanowicz.

point of view. *God* is the one who invented marriage. It was *His* idea in the first place, and He created it between one man and one woman. [30] Since *God is the ultimate authority*, even *if* the Catholic Church wanted to change it, she cannot. The Church knows that she does not have more authority than God. Neither I, nor the Church, nor anyone else on earth possesses that authority either. That's what I would say.

Girl #1: Woah! That was very interesting.

Boy #1: Yeah, *super* interesting.

Girl #2: You gave us so much to think about.

Boy #2: I totally agree with everything you just said, but can I ask a question to which I probably know the answer? Do you think our bodies are sacred and shouldn't be touched? Also, what do you think about changing your body?

Me: You mean like tattoos or something?

Him: Yes, that and/or plastic surgery. Are they sins?

---

[30] Some people state that homosexuality is genetic and that God made people this way, but no studies have confirmed this to date. Further, God did not make anyone that way; rather, He created marriage and sexuality between one man and one woman. Even if homosexuality *were* found to be genetic, that is not a justification for it or a sign that God approves it. Alcoholism and Clubfoot are said to be genetic too, just to name a couple of genetic abnormalities. I'm not necessarily comparing homosexuality to alcoholism but only using this example to show that no one would attempt to justify alcoholism *just because it's genetic.*

Me: My understanding is that it depends on the reason you get them. It seems reasonable that a person can get a tattoo, though perhaps not several of them. But again, what are the reasons?

I've known people who after being released from prison get a tattoo of Jesus or the cross on their arm. This is to remind them of God and the importance of staying on the right path. I don't see a problem with that. However, why would we need to cover the bodies that God gave us in tattoos? Tattoos are becoming an addiction for many people, a way to escape their problems, and that's never good.

Also, what if someone was in a car accident and had their face rearranged. They may need plastic surgery to fix it. There is nothing wrong with that. However, if someone is getting plastic surgery because they hate their body or feel unattractive, then they have not come to peace with who they are.

They are misinformed as to what true beauty really is. Therefore, I don't think plastic surgery would be an acceptable solution in those cases. Again, it depends on the reason in each scenario.

Boy #2: That makes sense. Honestly, I've sat here listening to you for a while, and I love how you don't just give lame, canned answers. I find your answers well thought out and rational. So, thank you!

Me: You're welcome. [Big smile]

Girl #3: Going back to marriage, don't you think that marriage is just a man-made institution created to civilize society?

Me: No, I believe God invented marriage long before societies and civilizations were ever created. It was His idea from the beginning. That's why we cannot change it even if we wanted to.

Girl #1: I have another question. Why is God a male?

Me: Actually, God is spirit. Therefore, He is not male or female, and in fact, He embodies the perfect qualities of both.

Girl #2: Then why do we call Him a male?

Me: While God is neither male nor female, we refer to Him as male because that's how He revealed Himself to us. He revealed Himself to us as a Father from all eternity. Also, when God came to earth in the person of Jesus Christ, He came as a male.

Girl #1: [Butting in] Yeah, but why a man instead of a woman?

Me: I have no idea. I'm not God. However, God is all wise and eternally perfect in everything. That was His perfect choice for reasons He alone knows. What we do know is that God did reveal Himself as Father. Perhaps one reason for this among others is that God sometimes embodies more male characteristics.

For example, when you look at the relationship between the Trinity (Father, Son, and Holy Spirit), the Father *initiates* the *love* between Himself and the Son giving *everything* to the Son. The Son *receives* that love fully and gives everything back to the Father. Their love is so infinite and perfect that it is a third person, the Holy Spirit.

Likewise, if you look at a married couple in the case of sexual love, the husband has to initiate the sexual act itself with his body part. He loves and gives everything he has to his wife (including his body, sperm, and sexuality). The wife receives his body and sexuality and gives herself back to him in total love. Their love is so strong that nine months later they give that love a name when the baby is born.

Because of his male body part, He is the one to give his body to her, and her body part receives his. By nature, a woman's body was made to receive. So, while God is not a sexual being in any way, our Father in heaven initiates love to us His children, and we the Church receive that love and give back to Him our whole selves. So, in *this* way, God is more like a man in that He initiates love to His people first and we receive it and give back to Him. That is also why we call the Church 'she' and 'her.'

Girl #3: [Interrupting me] You said the male initiates, but that's not always right, especially today. Of course the guy can initiate, but many macho guys expect the girl to do so and to be sexually available at all times. All of these machismo guys disgust me seeing how they treat women like porn stars for themselves. If they get a lot of women, they are "the man," but if women sleep around, they are called "sluts."

Me: I totally agree! A lot of what you say is true, and it's unfair. However, from a Christian point of view, that's not how it's supposed to be. It's not how God made it *nor* how He wants it. Any time we *use* someone else for our own selfish pleasure, it is a *perversion* of true love and sexuality, the opposite of the way God intended it to be.

When Jesus walked on earth, he reminded us of how God originally made man and woman; He made them *equal*. Men and women are supposed to be equals who serve each other and treat each other with the utmost respect. Men were made to treat women as princesses (which they are because women are all daughters of God who is the King).

A husband is supposed to serve his wife and even give up his life for her if need be.[31]  See how this is completely opposite from those men, who instead of serving women in love, they take everything from them selfishly. It's a perversion. And, it can go both ways. Remember: true love always seeks to serve and to give selflessly while lust is selfish and always seeks to take and to use.

Unfortunately, many of us men have been lied to about what

---

[31] See Eph. 5:25

it means to be a man, and we haven't been taught to properly love a woman. We men have this war raging inside of us. On one side, we want to properly love a woman and to be her knight in shining armor.

On the other side, we struggle with our weaker nature and trying not to use a girl for our own lust-filled selfish pleasure. Each and every man has this war, but a real man will work hard on freeing himself from these base passions of lust and work on bettering himself so that he can properly love and serve a lady, not use her.

Many women are also to blame though because they date these men who use them. I continually hear of women who like the "bad boys" and then complain constantly about them. Many women need to get their self-esteem and their standards out of the gutter and choose to date only those men who will treat them as they deserve. They may have to wait longer, but it's always worth the wait!

God calls us all, both men and women, to purify our hearts and false desires and to work toward being the best people we can be. There are many great men and women out there. There are many who are not. That's why it's important to *find the right person* in the first place and *not to settle* for anyone who will treat you less than you deserve.

Girl#3: That's so true! [Thinking silently] What about the Bible though? Doesn't it say that women have to be submissive to their husbands? Isn't that sexist?

Me: The part of the Bible you are referring to comes from Ephesians 5:21-33. First, you need to know that God made man and woman equal, and that's the way He wanted it. Second, this particular passage begins by saying that husbands and wives must be *submissive to each other*. Third, understand the context of the day. Women were usually subject to the man – sometimes mistreated. This was a consequence of the Original Sin of Adam and Eve.

However, St. Paul who wrote Ephesians was about to upgrade that mentality. He was, in effect, saying that *if* women were *supposed to be submissive*, then, here is the law for husbands. Husbands must love their wives *as Christ loved the Church* and gave up His life for her. In other words, a husband must love and serve his wife with all of his heart, putting her first, respecting her to the highest, and if need be, to die and give up his life for her. In that context, it seems like women have it easier. The bottom line though is: St. Paul was fixing the abuses and calling both men and women to equally love, respect, and serve each other.

Girl #3: Thank you. That makes sense!

*End Note:* Class was about to end, and so this ended the conversation. Everybody seemed satisfied with the answers and had nothing else to say. They all thanked me for coming and kept discussing and sharing on the way out of class.

# CHAPTER 14

✠

# Are You Two Going To Fight?

## *A Conversation with Two Atheists*

---

*Setting*: *An atheist and I were having a conversation about why she did not believe in God when a more ardent atheist overheard us talking and decided to come over and inform me of his atheism and as to why religion is irrational.*

Atheist #1: I'm an atheist.

Me: Oh really? I'm curious as to why?

Her: I don't know. Like, I believe in a higher power but not God.

Me: What does that even mean?

Her: Well, I believe that our spirits live on forever, and that everyone is eternal, but like there's no God.

Me: How can someone live forever if there is no eternal God?

Her: I don't really know. But, if there was a God, why would there be so much suffering in this world? If He was real, there *wouldn't* be suffering. Yet, there is suffering, so therefore, there is no God.

[As I'm about to respond, a far more militant atheist hears us talking about God. He walks over, plants himself in our conversation and just begins to give his views. Three other nearby people who wish to watch what's going down also come over to watch and listen.]

Atheist #2: I don't believe in God either. God's not real.

Person #3: Wait, you don't believe in God?

Atheist #2: Oh heck no. Definitely not. I think that religion is irrational.

Person #3: So wait, you don't believe in *anything*?

Atheist #2: Absolutely not. I believe in science. Science gives us actual answers while religion gives us none. All religions are irrational and contradict the rationally based logic of science.

Me: I love science too! But it's a fallacy to say that all religions are against the use of reason or contradict the logically based reason of science.

Atheist #2: [Annoyed and with a confused look on his face] Really? What religion in the world could possibly be rational? All the religions have their holy books and think their way is the only way. I don't know of any that find science acceptable, and I don't know any that can use logic or deductive reasoning.

Me: Well, I know of at least one – my religion.

Him: What religion are you?

Me: Catholic.

Him: Catholic? Are you kidding?

Me: Not at all. The Catholic Church has always supported science and believes that logic and reason are both absolutely necessary. In fact, one of the most recent popes wrote a whole encyclical on that very topic.[32] The Church has been emphatic that we cannot just believe blindly, but we must have reason alongside faith. That's why the Catholic Church does not fear science but supports it.

Atheist #1: Oh no! You're both making me nervous. You two are going to have a fight here or something, aren't you?

Me: A fight? Never!

Atheist #1: People always fight about religion. It gets too

---

[32] Pope John Paul II, *Fides et Ratio* (*On Faith and Reason*).

heated and confrontational.

Me: Some people might but watch and learn. Watch how two people can have a completely rational and peaceful discussion even though they completely disagree.

Atheist #2. Yeah, I agree with that. Back to the matter at hand though. The Catholic Church is not for science. Science contradicts religion.

Me: [Very nicely] Not at all. They both seek truth but do so in different ways. Religion seeks supernatural answers, trying to answer the question *who* made us and *why*, and science observes the physical realm attempting to answer the question of *how*. How did everything come about? Was it evolution or not? The Big Bang or not? That's the job of science to answer these questions.

If evolution is true, that's OK with the Catholic Church, as long as it's not viewed as a purely naturalistic process (meaning that everything happened by itself, randomly, without God who is deemed irrelevant). If the Big Bang is true, that's also fine with the Church. These views can be easily harmonized with what Catholics believe when properly understood.

Him: What? Come on. That's not true. The Catholic Church does not accept the Big Bang. It's too scientific for them.

Me: The Church does accept the Big Bang.

Him: No, no they don't.

Me: [Nicely] How are you going to tell me what *my* religion believes, hmm?

Him: I'm telling you, the Catholic Church is against science and the Big Bang.

Me: Fine! Then, let me ask you a question. Who first discovered the theory of the Big Bang? In other words, who was the first person to outline this theory?

Him: Oh. Ummm. Well... I actually don't know that off the top of my head.

Person #4: Einstein?

Me: Close. The person was a classmate of Einstein. His name was Fr. George Lemaitre. He was a Catholic priest *and* a scientist – a Belgian physicist to be exact. So, let me ask you a question. How could he be both a Catholic priest *and* a scientist if the Church was against science? Why were there many scientists, even priests and bishops, who were Catholic down through the centuries if the Church hated science?

Atheist #2: That's a good point. But, what about...

Me: Oh, can I add one more thing?

Him: Sure.

Me: Regarding the Church and science, few people know enough about history or about the Catholic Church to realize that the Vatican has one of the *oldest and largest* scientific observatories in the entire world. Why would that be if the Church and science were enemies?

Also, you probably didn't know that there are 35 craters on the moon named after Catholic priests. Why? Because of their extraordinary accomplishments in both math and science and because the Catholic Church gave more money toward science than all other institutions throughout the Middle Ages. Thus, the Catholic Church has contributed greatly toward the advancement and growth of science.

Him: Yeah, OK, I didn't know all that, but what about Galileo? The Church *was* against science at certain times. They condemned Galileo for proposing a theory that the Church was afraid of.

Me: Galileo wasn't condemned for scientific reasons.

Him: What?

Me: It's true.

Him: Everyone knows he was persecuted for holding to the theory of heliocentricity.[33]

Me: Well, not really.

---

[33] The belief that the sun, not the earth, is the center of the universe.

Him: No, that's a fact.

Me: Well, no... but let me try to explain it this way. Copernicus taught the same heliocentric model of the universe, right?

Him: Yes.

Me: So here is a question for you then: why was Galileo condemned while Copernicus wasn't? What did Galileo do that Copernicus did not do?

Him: Hmmm. I'm not sure. Probably because Galileo did not have permission and stepped on the Church's toes or something like that.

Me: Not really. Quite the opposite, in fact. He had full permission. In fact, the Church supported him 100% and even *funded his work* which enabled him to do his scientific research. Galileo was even good friends with the pope, Pope Urban VIII.

Many people in the Church, including the pope, loved Galileo's research and celebrated him for it. Some were even intrigued about his scientific work on the theory of heliocentricity, though cautious about it at the same time. *Not* because it was scientific or new but because they wanted to make sure he possessed enough evidence to sufficiently overturn belief in a geocentric universe.

Here is why. Roughly 2000 years ago, heliocentric theories

were presented but could not be proven. Moreover, Aristotle and Ptolemy had such powerful and persuasive arguments in their day that they utterly destroyed any heliocentric model of the universe for *over two thousand years*. Think about how long that is! Thus, it became common knowledge in the mind of every man that heliocentricity was false.

Nobody even argued for its cause; geocentricity is something everyone, *church and non-church people alike*, held as fact for thousands of years. So, to say that it might be wrong was like dynamite in the scientific community. This needs to be remembered when we come to Galileo.

Enter Copernicus. He began to discover evidence to the contrary. With this worldview in mind, you can see why many people were hesitant about it. Even non-Catholic, secular scientists were cautious of it at first too. Everyone was skeptical, as good science should be. Yet, Copernicus persevered, and at the urging of some Jesuits and even some bishops, he published a huge treatise on the subject that he dedicated to the pope.

Now, enter Galileo. The Church supported Galileo at first in this too, even funding him with large amounts of money. However, as I have said already, since this incredibly controversial theory was like dynamite in the scientific community, the Jesuits who were financing him didn't want to be embarrassed by Galileo pronouncing something as fact that he couldn't actually prove. Thus, they wanted him to have clear, sufficient evidence and to teach the heliocentric model as a *theory* until he possessed all the evidence needed.

We know today, that while Galileo made great strides in this work, complete evidence would not be produced until after his death with the advancement of certain technology. Copernicus taught this model solely as a theory. Galileo, however, went further and proclaimed it too eagerly as a fact. While he was correct in the end, he did not have sufficient evidence to prove it.

However, the much bigger problem came when Galileo began to claim that certain passages in the Bible were wrong, something Copernicus never did. Galileo had the audacity to leave the realm of science and try to pronounce on theological and religious matters. This is what got him into trouble.

So whether you agree with what the Church did or not, the Church's condemnation of Galileo was not for scientific reasons. The myths that Galileo was tortured and thrown into prison are more than false and have already been disproven.

The facts are these: he was put under house arrest with his own personal butler and all the latest conveniences. He was still allowed to do other scientific work. In fact, he came up with some of the greatest scientific discoveries of his life during this time. Note, that if the Catholic Church was against science, they would not have let Galileo keep working at all. Galileo died in good relationship with the Church, and here's a little known fact: both his daughters became nuns.

Him: Sooo, you said that Galileo was condemned for theological reasons and not scientific ones, for making himself more of an authority on the Bible than the Church.

Me: Correct.

Him. Well, I believe Galileo was right and that the Bible *is* wrong. I also believe that the Church is wrong. I mean, the Bible contradicts science. Christians actually believe that God created Adam and Eve directly while science teaches evolution, proving we came from primates. You Christians actually believe that the earth was created in seven literal days when science teaches that everything happened over billions of years.

Me: First, Galileo wasn't a studied theologian or a scholar, so he didn't understand the Bible well enough to pronounce as authoritatively on it as he attempted to. Second, while some modern religions and individuals might be against science, the Catholic Church is not, and she doesn't make the elementary mistake of interpreting everything in the Bible literally. There are many things in Scripture that are not literal.

For example, the Catholic Church does not teach that the days of creation are seven literal days. In fact, over 1600 years ago, St. Augustine, one of the most influential Catholic bishops in the history of the Church, taught that the seven days were symbolic. So, this is nothing new. After all, the Bible also states that one day for us is like a thousand days to

God and one day for God is like a thousand days to us.[34]  A *thousand* in the Bible means "a very long time," signifying that time for us is different than God's time, especially since He is outside of space and time.  So, the days in Genesis are not to be taken literally.

Him:  Well, some Christians believe this passage is literal.  And there are so many different Christian religions anyway that all contradict each other.  Did you know that there are more churches than restaurants and Starbucks here in America?  It's true.  Look at all the restaurants in the phone book.  You will find even more churches all claiming to be right.  So, who's correct?

Me:  You're right; there are a lot of competing churches.  But you have to remember, that while it all seems confusing to the modern person, it wasn't always this way.  At one time, there was only a single Christian Church, the Catholic Church, and it was that way for over 1000 years.  The two main splits came when the Greek Orthodox church separated themselves from the authority of the Pope in 1054 and when Martin Luther broke away from the Church in the 1500s both with no authority to do so.

So, for the most part, there was only one Christian teaching before Luther.  However, after Luther broke away from the Church, there were over 200 new religions by the time he died all claiming to go by the Bible and all claiming to be right.  Today, about 500 years later, there are tens of

---

[34] 2 Peter 3:8

thousands of Christian religions all following that pattern and all claiming to be right… thanks to Luther.

Yet, it wasn't always that way. There was only one Christian Church, the Catholic Church, for over 1000 years, and this is the Church Jesus started that has been there all along. The Catholic Church is like a huge Redwood tree that towers over countless little saplings in a forest.

Him: That makes sense to me. But, back to the Bible. What about Adam and Eve? How in the world is *that* true?

Me: Well, you have to understand what the Bible is. There are many different books in the Bible. Some are historical, others are poetry, and still others are apocalyptic, and so on. There are many different genres (sometimes even in the same book). So, you can't interpret them all the same way. That would be a huge mistake which is why many people misinterpret Scripture.

Regarding Genesis which you mentioned, biblical scholars tell us that the first 11 chapters of Genesis are more symbolic than literal, as far as genre is concerned. Not that these stories aren't true or are *merely* stories, but rather, instead of conveying the truth *literally*, they did so through story. Here's what I mean.

The writer of the first part of Genesis was not trying to write a science book, an encyclopedia, or to tell us *how* the world was made. You have to remember that the Bible is a spiritual book with the primary purpose of communicating spiritual truths. Therefore, the author's purpose was not to give a literal scientific description of how everything happened. Rather, he wanted to convey the truth that *God created everything.* And to do that, he used symbolic language.

For example, we don't believe there was an actual talking snake (not to mention the Bible never actually says that). Additionally, the names of the first two people probably weren't Adam and Eve. However, the devil really does exist, and he tempted the first two people. They really did sin against God and broke friendship with Him. Through their actions, they brought suffering and death into the world.

Exactly how it happened, we don't know. The author of Genesis was communicating that these things *did* happen to teach us important lessons, but not necessarily *how* it went down. Some people say these were only stories which never took place, but that's false and not what the Catholic Church teaches.

Consequently, if evolution is true, the Church says that Adam and Eve would have been the first two *people* to exist, what we call homo sapiens. We believe that God breathed a *rational* soul into man (as opposed to other animals who are not made in the image and likeness of God. They only have irrational souls).

Our *rational* soul endows us with free will and a rational intellect. Yes, we are animals, and yet much different than animals in that we are made in the image and likeness of God. Those are the truths the Bible is teaching us. There were two first people, a temptation, and a turning away from their Creator causing the need for them to be reconciled back to God. The Bible doesn't attempt to say *how* God made the world. That wasn't the author of Genesis' intention. If evolution is true therefore, it doesn't have to contradict the Bible.

Him: Actually, that makes sense. I can see that. But how do we even know that any of this is true in the first place. I mean, the Bible has changed like thousands of times, and there are countless versions of it.

Me: Actually, you may be surprised to know that the Bible hasn't changed as much as you'd think, nor has it been watered down through the centuries into a form that's unrecognizable, as many people assert. This is a common misconception though.

Him: No, it *has* changed, and there are many versions. You can't tell me there aren't different versions.

Me: Yes, there are many versions or translations (some better than others), but if you study the history and archeology of the Bible and the original languages, you will see that faithful translations haven't really changed as much as people think.

Him: Yes it has.

Me: [Nicely but firmly]: Look, we have some of the earliest Scriptures and versions of the Bible available to us. Some of these manuscripts are 1700 years old or more. Look at the Codex Vaticanus, for example. This is the earliest full Bible we have, and there are other partial manuscripts too that are even older.

If you match them up to the manuscripts we have today or those down through the centuries, they match up pretty closely. The actual evidence blows out of the water any argument that the Bible has been tampered with and can't be trusted. So, while modern English translations may differ, the original languages don't really differ very much.

Him: There's no proof of that!

Me: I just gave you the proof. Look up the Codex Vaticanus for yourself. It's there in black and white. Check it out.

Him: Ok, I will have to do that. I didn't know about the different ancient manuscripts.

Me: Oh definitely. Archeologists have different criteria for measuring how reliable ancient manuscripts are. Two ways are: the number of copies a document has and how close it was written to the original source.

Here are some examples: there are only two copies of the biography of Buddha.[35] So, if there are differences, all it reveals is that they differ from each other. There are not

---

[35] Information in this section came from, *The Case for Christ*.

enough copies to determine which parts are more authentic or which are the fraudulent additions or mistakes.

The Bible, on the other hand, has over 24,000 manuscripts in different languages that can all be studied, and they match up pretty closely. For instance, one version might say, "Jesus walked into a town" while another states, "Jesus walked into a village." In other words, the small changes that might occur are almost never so significant that they would change the meaning of a passage.

In addition, the first thing ever written on Buddha was about *600 years* after his death. The stories of Jesus were already being written about 15-20 years after His death. Which story do you think would be more accurate? The one written 600 years after the date? Or, the one written 20 years after by people who knew Him or His apostles personally?

Archeologists tell us that the closer a manuscript is written to the original source, the more accurate it will be. Naturally! So, we can accept the reliability of the New Testament because the Gospels (the stories of Jesus) were all written by eye-witnesses or by those who directly knew eye-witnesses. This makes the New Testament Gospels far more reliable than any and all other ancient manuscripts. They accurately communicate to us the stories and teachings of Jesus.

Him: Hmm. That's actually interesting. I didn't know that. Ya know, I like how the Catholic Church uses philosophy and reason in order to work toward logical interpretations and inductions. It doesn't seem like you just believe things blindly or take everything literally. Actually, the Catholic Church seems very reasonable to me in all this, and, I like talking to you about this stuff.

Me: [Speaking to atheist #1] See, you *can* discuss with those you disagree with in a kind and polite way. [Atheist #1 just shakes her head in agreement and smiles.]

Him: I just don't like the Christian religions that force their beliefs on others and translate the Bible like fundamentalists. Religious believers seem all about forcing their beliefs on others.

Me: I don't like that either. To be fair, many atheists and non-Christians also force their beliefs (or non-beliefs) on others too. They are not only intolerant many times but aggressive. The majority of Christians are great people. The Catholic Church, for example, is the largest charitable organization in the world.

Him: I did know that.

Me: Yes, we started orphanages, hospitals, and many other things to make the world a better place.

Him: I like that. I'm cool with that. It's just the people who force their beliefs on others that I have a problem with.

Me: With good reason, but they are more the minority. I do agree with you though about that; I don't like it either.

Him: [Joyfully. He has a whole different tone than when we first began talking.] Well, thanks for the conversation! I have actually enjoyed it. I like talking to people who are reasonable and know what the heck they're talking about.

Me: I have also enjoyed the conversation very much, and I hope we get to talk again sometime soon.

# CHAPTER 15

✟

# The Best Day Of Your Life

## *A Conversation about Life After Death*

---

*Setting:* *I was substitute teaching in a high school science class, and toward the end of the period a girl blurted out her fear of dying.*

Student #1: I'm afraid to die! [To some other students] Are you guys afraid to die?

Student #2: No.

Student #3: I'm not either. I don't care about death.

Student #1: [To student #3] What religion are you?

Student #3: I don't have one. I don't believe in anything.

Her: What about you Mr. Mercier? Aren't you very

religious? Don't you go to church and stuff?

Me: Yes. [Big smile]

Her: Awesome! So you can answer my questions then. So like, I'm really afraid to die. Doesn't death freak you out at all?

Me: No, not really.

Her: We'll, it freaks me out whenever I think about it. I mean when you die, that's it. Your body is dead, and you have to wonder if at the moment you die your mind knows it's even dead. Also, when you die you go into forever. Forever is a really, really, really long time. That doesn't freak you out at all?

Me: Occasionally the concept of forever is a bit intimidating, but I don't overly worry about it. After all, I believe in God, and I believe that heaven is really good place. It's a place of perfect goodness, happiness and bliss forever. Now that doesn't sound so bad, does it?

Her: It's just the concept that forever is *forever*. I can't even comprehend that. My grandmother died not too long ago. Do you think at the moment of her death she knew that she was dead? Do you think that when we die, our minds will know we're dead?

Me: Well, when we die, we go right to eternity, to heaven or hell. That's what I believe anyway as a Christian. However,

God made us to go to heaven with Him. So, I think our minds will be conscious one way or the other, but probably not here on this earth. We will certainly be able to know God.

Her: Will we be able to know other people up there as well?

Me: Yes! We will know all of our friends and family and everyone else who makes it. And we will never have to worry about pain, suffering, or death ever again. There will be only peace, love, and joy. Doesn't that sound nice?

Her: Sort of. But what is it like there? Are we even going to be able to interact with people? Will we even have a body?

Me: The Bible says that we will become even greater than the angels. Therefore, you will be able to fly; you'll possess super strength and intellect; you would be able to walk through walls, and so on. In other words, we will have perfected bodies in every way. You will not grow old, and your bodies will not become unhealthy. You will be perfect like angels, but even more glorious.

Her: Yeah, but will our bodies look the way they do now or like when we die as old people?

Me: We don't know for sure. What we do know is that we will have bodily perfection in every way. You'll recognize other people and be able to have relationships with them, though probably not in the same way as on earth. You won't need to sleep, to eat, or anything else because you will be perfect.

Her:  Yeah, but what if I want to eat ice cream?  I *love* ice cream!

Me:  Hmm.  What is your favorite food?

Her:  I only like about four foods.

Me:  Well, what's your favorite?  And also, what's your least favorite?

Her:  My favorite is probably pizza, and my least favorite is probably mushrooms.

Me:  So, your favorite food is pizza and your least favorite is mushrooms.  Pizza is way up here [I hold one hand up in the air over my head] and mushrooms are way down here [I hold my other hand much farther down to measure of the distance between the two.]  In heaven, everything you experience is going to be much better than pizza [I hold my hand way up], and even the best, most delicious things on earth will taste like mushrooms to you in comparison. [I hold my other hand way down.]

Her:  But what is heaven like?

Me:  Do you have a boyfriend?

Her:  Yes.

Me: How long have you been dating? Would you say you are in love with him?

Her: Yes! We have been dating for a year and a half.

Me: OK then. Try to imagine the one, single, greatest time you have *ever* had with him. Re-imagine and *feel* in your mind the emotions and the joy you had when your connection with him was the strongest. Try to remember what it was that made your "one greatest moment" so special. You probably never wanted that magical moment to end. Well, that's what heaven will feel like and much, much more. The best part is that it will *never* have to end.

Also, try to imagine some of the best, most fun times you've ever had in your life, times you wanted to go on forever. Maybe it was a sleepover at a friend's house. Maybe it was a family vacation. Maybe it was a trip to Six Flags or Disney World. Maybe it was an incredibly romantic date with your boyfriend. Try to remember how you felt during these times.

Remember the joy and happiness, the freedom and the carefree attitude you had. That's what heaven will be like. It will be amazing! The love you experience with your boyfriend might be strong, but it's nothing compared to the love you will have with God someday in heaven. Heaven is a relationship with the *source of all love*, God Himself. You will never be bored or unhappy even for a second in heaven.

Her: You won't be bored?

Me: Not even for a second. All the love, joy, peace, and good feelings possible will permeate your being and flood your soul at every moment fulfilling you in every way possible. That doesn't sound so bad does it?

Her: No, not so much when you put it that way.

Me: I think the unknown is always scary, and I can completely sympathize with that. We can often fear what we don't know, and that's totally understandable. I think it's because heaven is more of a vague notion or abstract idea for most people. Therefore, we usually have no idea what to expect. But we have nothing to fear if we stay close to God. He will watch over us and protect us. So, I think one thing that will help you greatly is to pray a lot and to try to develop a relationship with God. Do you pray every day?

Her: Sort of. Yeah, I guess so.

Me: It's tragic that many people just say prayers but don't often *pray* those prayers. They don't know how to go deep or make a connection with God. So, they pray, but it always feels empty. They just pray the same way they always have without deepening that relationship or coming closer to God. So, I would encourage you to deepen your prayer life. Bring it alive and make it more real! The more you come to know God, the more you will love Him, and the more you experience His love, the less fear you will feel.

Her: I do wish to have a deeper connection with God.

Me: You can! For example, how did you fall in love with your boyfriend? You got to know him! You talked to him, learned all about him, and got to know him as a person. The more you were able to get to know him, the more you liked him. Consequently, you desired to spend more time with him.

It's the same with God. In order to fall in love with Him and have that relationship, you must talk to Him and get to know Him! So, I am going to recommend that you do something that will help you in this. Do you have a Bible at home?

Her: Yes.

Me: Great! In addition to praying every day, I'm going to challenge you (or you can make it part of your prayer time) to read just *one chapter a day* of the Bible starting in the book of Matthew. Skip the opening list of names and begin with the birth of Jesus.

This will probably take less than 5 minutes or so a day to read, but it can change your life! Read one chapter a day stopping to think about and reflect on any part that may strike you or stand out to you.

Most people only pray quickly for a couple of minutes before bed every night, which is why it doesn't do anything and why they don't ever feel closer to God. If we want to get something out of prayer, we have to put a lot more into it. So, in reading the Bible and thinking about how it applies to your life, you will get to know who Jesus Christ is and how much He loves you.

In getting to know Him, it will help you to love Him and to deepen that connection with Him. I'd recommend trying to pray for 10-15 minutes a day in the beginning, even if it's not all in one sitting. So, definitely add reading the Bible to your daily prayer time. It will help. A lot! Staying close to God is the answer to not fearing death and to a peaceful life. What do you think about that?

Her: I really like that idea! I am totally going to do that!

Me: Awesome!! If you ever have any questions, you can ask me anytime. [Smile]

Her: Thank you so much. I *really* appreciate it.

Me: No problem! I'm glad that we had the chance to talk today. [Big smile]

Her: Me too!

# CHAPTER 16

# How God Changed My Life

---

## *In This Chapter:*

1. *Why I believe in God*
2. *How He changed my life*
3. *How to share your faith with others*

I grew up in a Catholic family and have always believed in God. Growing up, I prayed every day, went to church on Sundays, and even attended Catholic school for most of my life. However, around the beginning of my teenage years, questions began to surface in my mind about the Catholic faith. Unfortunately, I rarely received any satisfying answers. Instead, people just told me to "have faith" or, "It's a mystery." These were not good answers though and certainly not helpful.

In high school, more doubts and questions surfaced. No matter how much I prayed, it seemed that God never answered my prayers. I prayed for many things which I deemed very important and yet didn't see any results.

Therefore, I figured that either God was not real, or He *was* real, but He did not care about me. Or perhaps, He was an angry, big-bearded old man bazillions of light years away, and it took forever for my prayers to reach Him.

Obviously, I didn't know who God really was at the time. Sometimes I believed strongly. At other times, it felt like tossing prayers into the air to someone who wasn't there for me. Rarely did I feel close to God or feel like I had any kind of a connection with Him.

All this time, the stress of high school and family life caused me to become deeply depressed and angry. While I acted normal in school, after school was a different story. I began to dress in all black from head to toe many times and to carry weapons in my clothes among other things.

Writing poems helped me to verbalize my feelings a bit. After a while though, the poems became very dark, and I wrote about hurting and even killing people. They eventually became graphic and deranged. In my mind, I was becoming like a "Columbine"[36] type kid. If my parents had not raised me with religion and morality, I may have gone down the path of no return!

---

[36] Two angry kids in Columbine, Colorado came to school with guns and shot up their school killing many.

The truth is that I was sad, lonely, and incredibly depressed much of the time not knowing how to deal with my feelings. I never got into sex or drugs. Having fun with friends and playing insane amounts of video games were my "drugs of choice." However, even these were only temporary solutions to the cry of my heart. Neither of them could fix my problems in the end nor take away my pain. Even when I did have girlfriends, I still felt empty inside, especially when they were not around.

In short, I hated myself and my life a lot. For seven years, I did not even look in a mirror because I *hated* what I saw. I thought myself to be the ugliest person on planet earth. My self-esteem was rock bottom, life stunk, and I was just tired of it all.

My life would not remain dark forever though, and it was during my third year of college that it would change forever. Little did I know that the Lord God of the universe was going to reveal Himself to me, rock my world, and *radically transform my life for the better*!

## God Transforms My Life!

After attending a two-year college, I reluctantly ventured out to Franciscan University of Steubenville, Ohio, one of the best Catholic colleges in America. At this time, I swore like a sailor, told dirty jokes, vowed not to "pray if I didn't want to," and made fun of all the "holy rollers" there. Despite the bad attitude, this college is where God decided He would change my life.

The Lord Jesus had great mercy on me, and it was there at Franciscan University where I encountered Him in a very powerful and very real way. My experiences of God were unmistakable and life-changing. I wasn't looking for these experiences and never thought they would happen to me. These encounters helped me to *know* God (Jesus) instead of just knowing *of* Him, to believe in Him, and to *know* that He existed. Most of all, I learned His immense love for me.

Perhaps these powerful experiences were due to the fact that I had prayed every single day of my life *in spite of* all my doubts and difficulties. I never gave up on God, and He never gave up on me. Additionally, I prayed a Rosary (a *very* powerful prayer) every single day throughout high school and mostly through college. As dark as life got, I never let go of God or my faith.

Not only was my mother praying for me to Jesus and sacrificing for me too, day after day, year after year, but my heavenly mother Mary was also praying for me to Jesus with her powerful intercession. So, even though I went through doubts and difficult times, I always prayed, attended church, and tried to seek God *even when it didn't make sense.*

For all of the above reasons, and perhaps others, I believe God worked very powerfully in my life. That is why it is so important to seek God with all of our hearts and to never give up even in times of doubt, fear, hardships, trials, or the catastrophes of life. That is why it is so important to pray each and every day and to work on going deeper with God.

Jesus made His divine presence and power known to me. In a real way, the Lord Jesus transformed me from the inside out. He took my pain and confusion and replaced it with abundant peace and freedom. He took all of my anger and hatred and gave me an *overflowing love for everyone*, even those I had previously hated. He took all my sadness and years of depression and replaced them with a contagious joy and a bubbling happiness!

Finally, He took all the pieces of my broken heart, healed them, and made me into a completely new person. He gave me new life. That was almost 20 years ago, and ever since that time, I have never hated or even strongly disliked anyone. That's the power and grace of God working in someone's life! I've learned that we have to stay faithful to God in all seasons. Sometimes He takes a long time before choosing to make a big change in our lives, but there's always a good reason, and it's *always worth the wait*!

Unfortunately, going back home during school breaks was miserable. My family and friends didn't understand my new life or what had happened. My friends often made fun of me for being religious and convinced me to return to my former sinful lifestyle. Back at college, I would repent and return to Jesus. The awesome thing about Jesus is that He always forgave me completely and unconditionally. He always took me back. This was a cycle that happened a few times over, but each time I grew stronger and resisted sin longer. He *loved* me, and I *felt* that love strongly and tangibly.

One day, it struck me just how much Jesus loved me and how

*unconditional* God's love was for me. No one else had ever loved me like that, and no one else could give me the deep and abiding peace, joy, and freedom that I received and experienced in Him.

Consequently, I decided to make a concrete decision to live my life totally for Jesus. Throughout my life, I have sinned thousands and thousands of times, and yet, God has always forgiven me. He knew all of my sinfulness and still loved me. He knew me at my worst and still chose to take my punishment for sin by dying on the cross for me. How awesome is that! Reflecting on this, I realized that Jesus was the ultimate fulfillment of our life and infinitely worth living for! Only He could give me the ultimate happiness and satisfaction my heart was searching for.

Thus, I made the decision to give my life to Jesus promising that I would never return to my old sinful ways of living. That was over almost 20 years ago, and I have never gone back. Rather, I have lived for God every day since and my life has been amazing! Never ever has my life been happier. Now, this is not to say that it's all been easy or that I don't have any problems. Sometimes, life is hard! Very hard.

However, it's so different now. When things get tough, I have *hope*. I have an amazingly loving God who is always there through everything helping me through my problems and making me the best I can be. He is like a rock one can hold on to in the mist of crashing waves. Without that rock, we would surely perish in the dark, chaotic storms of life. Bottom line: Jesus is the answer that every person is looking for whether they realize it or not. He is the fulfillment of our every desire and the only answer to our heart's cry.

Some people retort, "If religion works for you, that's great, but it's not for me." God is the creator of *everyone* and the *source of all happiness*. Therefore, nobody can find ultimate peace or happiness without God – or eternal life. Thus, He *is* necessary for everyone whether they realize it or not.

Most people who "tried God" or "tried religion" and found it lacking usually did it *their* way, not God's. They did what felt comfortable and avoided the rest. Or, they just went through the motions or gave the minimum amount possible. Imagine if we did that in our relationships or our marriages.

People who believe that following God and Christianity is slavery are very misinformed, don't understand their faith, or have done it wrong. Living our faith out of guilt, fear, or because you feel that you *have to*, doesn't help us get us closer to God. Our faith should not be a bunch of boxes to check or a bland set of rules to follow.

Rather, it's a relationship with the God of the universe who loves us so immensely that it's hard to imagine. Much of the problem is that we don't think we are worthy and so will not let God love us or forgive us. My life has been made whole and is infinitely better because of Jesus. Far from being slavery, God has freed me, given me great joy, and truth be told, I've never felt so *alive* and *happy*!

Jesus is a personal God who is worth having a relationship

with. Christianity can be tough, and there are still struggles, but any time difficulties arise in life, it's nice to have a faithful friend and Savior who will never leave your side. He alone can turn curses into blessings, darkness into light, mistakes into redemption, and sadness into joy. That's why I love God and live for Him every day. That's why I am wholeheartedly and unapologetically Catholic!

## Learning My Catholic Faith – The *Hard* Way

After my powerful experiences and inner healing, there was no doubt that I loved God with all my heart. However, I could not explain or defend my faith which would soon become obvious. One day in Pittsburgh, I came across two Jehovah's Witnesses on a street corner. They didn't waste time with pleasantries but immediately began to inform me that Jesus wasn't God (as Christians believe), and that the Catholic Church was an invention of the pagan Emperor Constantine.

While I felt the Jehovah's Witnesses were wrong, all I could muster were subpar answers void of good facts. Each time that I attempted to respond to them, they buried me with a multitude of Bible verses and explanations. My faith was shaken that day. Like a starving person desperately seeking food and water, I desperately wanted to learn the answers to their questions, to know *why* I was Catholic, and to discover if my Catholic beliefs were correct. After all, how did I know Catholicism was true? Was I just Catholic because my parents were? And, were they only Catholic because their parents were, and so on?

Unlike many people who choose to leave their religion without researching it first, I decided to look up the answers to these questions and to explore all of their objections. The following week, I told the Jehovah's Witnesses what I had learned only to have more objections thrown in my face. This happened every week and always ended with me having to go research more answers. This went on for about 6 months, and I really started to grow in an understanding of my faith. I became better at sharing it too and even made them have to think sometimes.

Around that same time, I ran into some fundamentalist Protestants who bluntly informed me that Catholics were on their way to hell for worshiping Mary, for trying to work their way to heaven, and for accepting many other false teachings "not found in the Bible." Needless to say, more research was necessary. Like the Jehovah's Witnesses, each time I brought back answers that I had researched, these fundamentalists would beat me over the head with more objections and condemnations.

Book after book, CD after CD, question after question, and even taking some theology courses, all really helped my knowledge to explode. It was *awesome* to discover that there were great answers out there for all my questions which also provided backing for my beliefs. It became addicting! The more I learned, the more everything made such perfect sense, more than I ever thought possible. I wanted to keep learning!

Like a puzzle with all the pieces coming together to form a single picture, so my Catholic faith was coming together in my mind and began to crystalize and make a ton of sense. I could not get enough! Thanks be to God, I also became exceedingly proficient in sharing my faith with others and answering their questions and objections.

That was almost 20 years ago, and I still *love* to learn, dive deeper, and grow in my understanding. This learning is what helps take our faith from *super boring* to *super exciting*! This is one reason why I chose to be a Catholic speaker, author, and retreat leader, teaching the Catholic faith professionally to others.[37] My ardent desire is to help Catholics to learn and love their Catholic faith, to have that faith come alive, and to help them be able to articulate their beliefs effectively so they do not have to be as awkward as I was when encountering those who have questions.

My relationship with Jesus is like watching a fantastic movie that you can't wait to share with others. After all, we share

---

[37] When people hear me preach on the Catholic faith, they often long to "explain the faith like I do." When they hear me enter into discussions with other religions and expound my beliefs, they despair that they could never defend Catholicism like that. Imagining that I was born with this gift, they resign any hope in gaining it. However, I hope that my story has made it perfectly clear that I *learned* how to defend my faith *the hard way* through a lot of trial and error and by sheer determination. An atheist friend of mine in college, for example, made me cry because she bombarded me with so many objections that I could not answer. [Love ya, Violet!] But, I didn't give up trying. Other people too have made me feel silly or even stupid for how little I knew. But, I did not give up. Thus, with time and practice, anyone can learn to share the faith even if they don't feel capable. Remember, God doesn't usually *call the qualified;* He *qualifies the called.* What you need is the desire and trust!

our favorite books, foods, TV shows, movies, video games, vacation destinations, and many other things that we really enjoy. The more we relish something, the more we *can't wait* to share it with those around us. That's how my relationship with Jesus is. He changed my life, and I love to share that with others. I never preach at others or force it on them, but I also don't hesitate to share the joy my life has because of Him. Nor, do I shy away from defending my faith. If I do, I pray and beg God for more courage.

That's where I am today, but it was a long journey to arrive here. Back in my senior year of college, I made the decision to share Jesus with as many people as possible and to share what He had done in my life. I was positive that my excitement would be contagious and that my family and friends would want their lives transformed too. I was wrong! Once again I had to learn the hard way. If you have all the right answers but don't know how to share them properly, then all the answers in the world won't help reach anyone.

## Learning the Most Important Lesson of My Life

Most of my friends and family were not open to what I had to say. They mistakenly thought that I was just "preaching" to them while others thought that I had gone off the deep end. In hindsight, I probably possessed more desire than tact and could have gone about it more prudently – a skill that would be acquired later on. I had a ton of raw zeal but did not know how to share it properly or effectively. This helps to demonstrate that *how* we say something is as important as *wha*t we say.

I evangelized (shared my faith) with great joy but often met resistance. At first, I responded to this repeated resistance with disappointment and even sadness. It felt like running repeatedly into a brick wall. What I desired was for someone to understand my experience and to share my excitement, but they didn't – and did not care to.

I had become more adept in sharing my Catholic faith with people of different religions, but many times conversations became intense. I had enthusiasm but little tact or patience. Consequently, these discussions became heated many times, especially when they attacked me. I would meet fire with fire beating my opponents over the head with "the truth" as if it were a sledgehammer. Sometimes, I would get so angry that I would lose my temper, and it would take me a long time to calm down.

This all came to a climax one day as I was evangelizing in Pittsburgh. Many of my classmates were praying in front of an abortion clinic. They were praying that the mothers who entered the clinic would make the right decision and give their child the gift of life. Of course, these heartfelt students also prayed for the mothers and offered them any aid they could.

On the other side of the street, Christian fundamentalists would gather to yell out to these women that they were going to hell. These fundamentalists were an embarrassment to the rest of us Christians. To make matters worse, they enjoyed telling us Catholics that we were going to hell too. For this reason, I made it my job to go over there and distract them by speaking to them about the Catholic faith.

Out of the blue one day, a woman came over to me. As soon as I met her, I knew she was angry. You could feel the anger oozing out of every pore of her body. She began to yell in my face about how, "I had no right to be at an abortion clinic because I was a man," and so on.

Instantly becoming enraged, I reacted in a way that was inflammatory matching her anger blow for blow. Also, I may have blurted out something about her going to hell. As we yelled in each other's faces, my temper gage was about to explode causing me to yell at her and then walk away in a fury. I called back, "Have fun on Judgment Day!"

A little while later, I returned to the same spot, and what I saw would forever change the way I shared my faith. My soft-spoken friend Bridgette was there. She was sitting Indian style on the sidewalk holding this same lady in her lap. The angry lady was literally lying on the cement with her head on Bridgette's lap, and she was crying her eyes out. Bridgette calmly stroked this woman's hair as she sobbed uncontrollably.

My mouth hit the ground. "Bridgette can't explain her faith to save her life," I thought to myself. "How in the world did she get through to this lady? What did I do wrong?" In hindsight, it is shocking that I couldn't see how damaging my words and actions were *even* if she "deserved it."

In that very moment, God hit me like a ton of bricks. It was a lightning bolt moment, and He floored me right then and there. I had a revelation, and everything became crystal clear. Bridgette did not preach. She did not yell. She did not scream or even lecture. She probably didn't say much at all. Yet, whatever she said or did caused this lady to break down (in a good way). Bridgette did not judge her or condemn her but just loved her – something this lady desperately needed. Bridgette showed the immense love of Jesus to her, and that is what worked. She also had mercy and compassion, two traits Jesus Himself would have had.

Sadly, I "the professional" gave this woman a horrific example of Catholics and of Jesus. She could have been turned away from God forever because of me. If only everybody could have seen with what gentleness and compassion Bridgette stroked this lady's hair. Her love was simple but earthshattering. Sincere and powerful. She showed this hurt, angry woman God's unconditional love and did more in a few minutes than I could have done in a few years with my horrible example.

That day taught me one of the greatest lessons of my entire life, bar none. Namely, that love is the most important thing in the world *and* in sharing the faith. Period! Love changes minds and transforms hearts. Love reveals God and breaks down walls. It accepts people as they are, and it cares for them and their souls passionately *even* if they have no plans to change or convert. This love creates the necessary soil that allows people to change and grow in their own time when they are ready. It is indispensable!

Love sees *everyone* as a *child of God,* not as a pathetic heretic who needs to convert. That attitude is from the devil. Anger, frustration, judgmentalism, annoyance, and all the rest are *not from God.* These show defects in our character and how much work we need to do in our own spiritual lives. As Fr. Michael Scanlon used to say paraphrasing Scripture, "God resists the proud... even if they're right!"[38]

This whole incident was life altering for me immediately and permanently changing the way I shared the faith. Since that day, I have never yelled at anyone or become angry or un-Christ like with anybody. While some people still yell and condemn *me*, I am able to love them deeply and see what they can become – just as God saw what I could become. I completely realize that this is a grace from God. This great love for everyone has without a doubt made all of my evangelization efforts more powerful and infinitely more effective.[39] It has made me the evangelist I am today.

---

[38] See James 4:6

[39] The only exception to this came many years later with the dawn of online discussion forums. On the internet, people are fiercely derogatory, angry, immature, hostile, insulting, emotional, and verbally abusive. While cowardly hiding behind their little screens, they vomit slurs and condemnations without a care that you are a person who has feelings and are made in God's likeness and image. The tendency is to be defensive and respond hastily back in some less than Christian way. However, I brought this to the Lord Jesus, and He has helped me (and continues to help me) to love them, to have patience, to see them as persons who are hurting or insecure, and to share my Catholic faith in charity, humility, and sincerity. Again, this *always* has a far more powerful impact than just responding emotionally and rudely off the cuff. Where there is no love, there is no godliness or holiness!

Anger, frustration, and beating people over the head is indicative that a person still needs more conversion in their own lives *even* if they go to daily Mass or possess a lot of book knowledge. Having great love and being a joy-filled example of Christ is far better than possessing a wealth of knowledge or advanced apologetics skills (though you need both for sure). Love is *the* most important thing.

With that being said, there are many wishy-washy religions and "spiritual" people today who assert that love is *all* we need. They claim that we must love and then "rid ourselves of all commandments and doctrines." This is blatantly false. God is not only love, but He is also truth. Therefore, love without truth is a lie, and keeping that truth to yourself is not truly loving. Jesus Christ Himself gave us truth to set us free, and it would be unloving *not* to share it.

Thus, having a deep knowledge of our Catholic faith and an efficiency in sharing it are both very important. We need to learn our faith well, hone our skills in apologetics, study other people's objections, and learn how to answer them effectively. The more we practice sharing our faith, the easier it will become. The more we turn to God, the more He will change our hearts and bless our endeavors. For tips and techniques on how to share the faith more effectively, see Part II of this book.

# Closing Remarks

*For Agnostics, Skeptics, and Non-Believers:*
My sincere hope is that this book has touched you in some way and has helped to answer some of your questions. I pray that it has opened up a desire (no matter how small) to know God more and seek Him in your life. While you may still have questions, it's important to know that learning is a lifelong process and a person does not need to have every question answered in order to have an understanding of God, to believe in Him, or to make a decision to follow Him. You just need enough evidence to see that belief in God is reasonable and rational. Over time, more and more evidence will follow.

If you feel that many of your questions were answered and the God question makes sense, I would ask you to consider praying to Him and perhaps even making a concrete decision to follow Him more in your life. To help you with this, begin praying every day *even* if it feels awkward at first or doesn't seem to do much.

If you still have doubts, consider praying to God for more faith and continue to do more research. Remember, *faith is a gift* from God, not something we just inherit by studying enough – though that does help. If you need more faith, ask daily for it! Also, reading the New Testament of the Bible will help you a lot. I highly recommend that.

If you are interested in dating someone but never take the time to talk with them, you will never get to know who they are. It is the same with God. That is why praying, reading the Bible (especially the New Testament), and studying the faith is so important. Those who humble themselves and tell God they are in need of Him will find Him much faster.

Even though there is a lot of good evidence for God's existence and good answers for other religious questions, some people still choose not to believe. They choose unbelief, not because there's no evidence, but because they consider following God to be "too much work." Or perhaps, they want to live life "their own way," or don't want to submit to a higher authority, and so on.

However, God *is* the ultimate authority, and we will all have to answer to Him in this life or the next. If Atheists are right, no one will ever know when they die. If Christians are right, *everyone* will know, and the truth will be perfectly clear to all. The existence of God is the most important question of our life, and it is the one we want to get right.

We must remember that God made every one of us and *has a plan for our lives* to make us happy! I hope that by seeing what God has done in my life, it will inspire you also to desire Jesus and His life-changing love for you.

### *For Believers:*

If you are already a believer, my hope is that this book has increased your faith, helped to bring you even closer to God, and has provided you with a greater knowledge, clarity, and understanding regarding God and your Christian beliefs. I also pray that you feel sufficiently inspired and equipped to be able to speak about your faith and defend it when the time comes.

If you sense that a fire has been placed in your heart along with a desire for others to know the truth, please share this information with them. God may be calling you in a special way to share His love and truth with others.

# PART II:

# SHARING YOUR FAITH

# The Top 10 Evangelization Dos and Don'ts

Evangelization! It does not matter how much knowledge a person has if they do not present the information in a way someone can understand or in a way that turns them off. It's not just *what* we say, but *how* we say it! Below are some essential tips on how to share your faith and how not to.

Apologetics and evangelization is a cultivated art! It takes practice, trial and error, success and failure. Most people are afraid to try due to a fear of failure. But, this is a form or pride where we put all the pressure of success on ourselves rather than realizing that it is God's job to change other people's hearts and minds. We are just His instruments – the widows that allow His Light to shine through. The more we give our endeavors to God and trust Him, the more He will work in and through us. Our job is to plant seeds, and it is God's job to water those seeds and to make them grow. Evangelization is not about winning or losing arguments but reaching and winning souls.

If evangelization is something you are nervous about, start small. For example; if someone at work asks what you did over the weekend, among other things, tell them that you went to church (instead of conveniently leaving that detail out). You are not being pushy, and this may open up a friendly door for you to discuss God or religious matters sometime in the future. However, if your evangelization *is* abrasive, forceful, or aggressive, you are doing it wrong. Below are some quick tips for sharing your faith. Read them through from time to time to keep them fresh in your mind.

*DOs:*

1. Love!  Have great love and compassion for those you speak to regarding the faith.  Both a love and concern for souls is central for successful evangelization!  Remember that Jesus calls us to love everyone without exception, especially those who need it most.  We must pray often for great charity so that we can be a shining example of Christ to others.  This flows from knowing Jesus' love for you and from having a deep relationship with Him.

2. Understand others.  Try to understand where another person is coming from.  This is crucial.  Don't just *hear* what they are saying but try hard to *understand* what they really mean, where their beliefs are coming from, and *why* they believe what they do.  In other words, don't just listen with your ears but with your heart too.

   Many times what people say is only a surface argument and not the real problem.  Their real issue is often much deeper, and until you understand it, you will never get through to them.  For example, if someone is emotionally charged and vehemently attacks the Catholic Church for the Crusades or for other bad events in history, then they have probably been hurt by the Church in some way.  It may not be about the Crusades at all.

   Yes, they are spurting out arguments, but the real issue is an emotional one that is disguised as an intellectual one.  Usually the person himself doesn't even realize what the root issue is, so we must listen well and try to find it.  Don't diagnose people verbally!

Also, do not miss what others are saying because you are trying to form a response in your mind. That is important. Listen and understand first. Ask questions in order to understand more. Then respond.

3. Ask questions! Asking questions is a superb form of evangelization and is crucial for the process. Don't ask just for the sake of stumping them; rather, make your questions sincere. This can be your best evangelization technique if you learn how to master it. See the conversation about Aliens in chapter 4.

4. Be sincere. Be humble, and do not be afraid to admit that you don't know an answer or need to look something up.

5. Learn critical thinking skills. Learn how to sift through a person's argument to find the holes and flaws. Learn the arguments of the other side in advance and research the best way to respond. This will significantly help you to develop this skill more.

6. Clear up misconceptions. Help people to understand what we actually believe as Christians, as opposed to what they *think* we believe or what other people have incorrectly told them. This is one of the most important and helpful evangelization techniques.

7. Have a personal testimony! Have a 30 second to one-minute witness of what God has done in your life and how your life is better because of Him. This means you'll have to think about it and take some time to put it

together. Be *joyful* when sharing it. Testimonies can often get through to people when intellectual arguments do not. Having a testimony is the easiest way to evangelize because you're not "preaching doctrine" to anyone but only sharing your story – like a good movie you saw. (See my 30 second testimony – Page 28)

8. Find common ground. Sometimes it helps to begin by focusing on those things you have in common and then discuss the differences from there.

9. Persevere. If one argument doesn't work, try another. Do not get frustrated if people don't understand right away... or at all. Pray for patience. A good evangelist would wait patiently all day if it meant the other person could grasp what they're saying. Conversion does not take place over night. It's a process. People who are seeking immediate conversions have the wrong motives for sharing the faith. They care more about winning an argument than winning a soul.

10. Practice – in little ways or in bigger circumstances. Try. Fail. Try again. Repeat. Keep growing each time! You have to put yourself out there and try! Then, learn from your experiences (for good or bad) and try again.

11. *Pray*! Pray for yourself and for everyone you have spoken to and will speak to in the future. If you do not pray, all of your efforts are in vain!

***DON'Ts:***

1. Don't be prideful, haughty, or have a holier than thou attitude. These are never from God.

2. Don't be judgmental or critical of others. Now, we may be able to judge certain *actions*, but not hearts, intentions, or a person's salvation.

3. Don't get heated or angry. Keep composed and never lose your temper. Remember, you represent the Lord Jesus, and so your thoughts, words, and actions must reflect that. Therefore, it is necessary that we rid ourselves of all sassiness, sarcasm, or bitterness.

4. Don't be impatient. Evangelization takes time, and sometimes a very long time. Some of the greatest conversions in life take the most time. If we find ourselves getting impatient, it's probably because *we* are trying to convert a person rather than recognizing that it's the job of the Holy Spirit to bring about someone's conversion. We get frustrated that they are not listening, but there are many obstacles and blocks in other people's lives that we must consider. Furthermore, God works in His own time. Don't kill the flower by trying to rip it open in order to make it bloom quicker. Develop patience!

5. Don't get defensive which can lead to #1, #2, or #3.

6. Never insult, call names or degrade anybody, even if they do it first.

7. Never yell or scream, and don't get frustrated.

8. Don't respond fire with fire, and don't take on other people's emotions. Stay calm and keep yourself emotionally separated from the other person. If they start getting upset and aggressive, that doesn't mean you need to. Our goal is to always be a good example of Christ even if they get out of line. A good example always speaks far louder than words.

9. Don't try to do the impossible. Sometimes people will attack you or attack the Church with one wrong argument after another. They are rude and won't let you get a word in. Realize that sometimes, no matter what you say, it will be shot down. They may also insult you or your faith. Remember, you cannot correct someone who doesn't want to be corrected or help someone who refuses to be helped. When you realize that they don't want to listen, you may walk away and just pray for them. Love them, but *don't be a doormat.* You do not have to stay and talk. Sometimes, we must take the way of humility and realize that praying for the person is the best option, especially when nothing we say or do seems to compute with them. Prayer is always more powerful in these situations.

10. Don't rely on yourself. Offer everything you do to God. Give to God each person you evangelize to. *He* is in charge. It is *He* who will do all the heavy lifting and bring about any change!

# For Those Who wish To Evangelize:

*Prayer and Spirituality:*  It is absolutely essential to have a good spiritual life where the life and grace of God can work in and through you.  So:
- Pray every day for at least 30-60 minutes or more.
- Work on virtue (humility, kindness, patience, etc.).
- Strive to be *holy*.  Don't be a hypocrite – preaching one thing and living another.  Do not tell others to dress modestly if you yourself curse like a sailor.  Don't look down at others for having sex before marriage if you yourself are addicted to porn, and so on.
- The closer you are to God, the more His light can shine through you.  The more you want to change the world, the more you first need to change yourself.


*Study Apologetics*:  The art of explaining and defending your faith.
- Read the Bible often (preferably daily).  Especially focus on the New Testament.
- Be familiar with the Catechism of the Catholic Church.  Or for teens: try reading *YouCat* for starters.
- Read good Catholic apologetics books and materials.  (See some suggestions at the end of this book).
- Listen to apologetics talks, CDs, podcasts, etc.
- Study some church history and be familiar with some of the common objections.
- Learn the arguments from the other side and the best ways to answer them!

# Some Final Thoughts

If you put these tips and techniques into practice, you will be well on your way to explaining your faith with more fluidity and effectiveness. In addition, you will lead other people toward God and back to the Church, which is not always easy, especially when it comes to friends and family.

*A Final Note in Dealing with Difficult People:*

Famous atheist Richard Dawkins has instructed his cult followers to insult Christians and to *laugh in their faces.* In stark contrast, Jesus Christ instructs *His* followers to love everyone *even* people who mock them. So, let us follow Christ and not our pride in evangelizing and never stoop to the low level of Dawkins or his followers.

Even if someone comes nose to nose with you and laughs out loud in your face, you must humble yourself and say a quick prayer for them interiorly. You may even retort sincerely, "May God bless you my friend," as you smile and walk away. That will be more powerful than all the words you could think of in response. Your whole witness as a Christian will be treated as a joke if you stoop to their level.

If you find it humiliating, think of Christ on the cross. Are you greater than He? Jesus was utterly humiliated, and He is our example. We must also remember that this humiliation led to the greatest victory of all time! This humiliation and surrender to God is also how the early Catholics took over the whole Roman Empire when that same empire was trying to wipe them off the face of the earth. They humbled themselves, prayed fervently, and loved passionately. God did the rest!

I know from experience that skeptics and non-believers don't always come to believe in God due to my arguments alone, but rather because of the joy and authenticity that radiates through me even when they are rude. These skeptics see something in me they are missing in their own lives.

That's why a good prayer life is necessary and indispensable for holy living and to have God's grace working in us. The angriest and most hardened people we meet are the ones who need our love and kindness the most. The angrier someone is, the more they are crying out for God's love without even knowing it.

With that being said, there are many good, logical, well-thought-out reasons for believing in God. It's up to each of us to find them, learn them, and share them with others. So, study your faith! Read books, blogs, or websites. Make sure *you* understand what you believe and why. Always be prepared to defend your faith, and feel free to engage in dialogue about it.

Keep in mind that any skeptic, atheist, or agnostic can come to God at any time. In fact, some of the most stubborn and obstinate atheists have become believers. For example, Antony Flew was said to be the most notorious atheist in the world last century. However, even he converted to faith in God after decades of arguing fiercely against His existence.

How did he come to believe? People persevered in praying for him and engaging him in dialogue about the faith. At one point, Mr. Flew decided to look at the evidence for God with an open mind for the first time in his life. He saw something He never expected to see… actual evidence for God that was rational and made sense! If this fiercely stubborn man can change, *anyone* can!

Look up the many atheists who have become Christians. See how happy and complete their lives are because of God. Hold that as an image in your mind when speaking to difficult people, and let it be a model of hope.

Now, it is your turn. It is time to go shine your light in a dark world, a world that desperately needs the love and life-transforming message of Jesus Christ. So, pray for boldness and courage. Pray for the gifts of the Holy Spirit. Pray for abundant love, joy, and holiness. Pray to be a good and faithful witness.

*May God bless you on your journey!*

# Sources Referenced

Aquinas, Thomas, *Summa Theologica*, Vol. 1: Notre Dame, IN: Ave Maria Press, 1948.

*Catechism of the Catholic Church*, New York, Doubleday Publishing, 1994.

D'Souza, Dinesh, *What's So Great About Christianity*, Washington DC: Regnery Publishing, 2007.

*Holy Bible: Revised Standard Version,* San Francisco: Ignatius Press, 1966.

Kiser, Keith and Tammi, *The Incredible Gift*, Huntington, IN: Our Sunday Visitor, 1996.

Kreeft, Peter, Tacelli, Ronald K, *Handbook of Christian Apologetics*, San Francisco: Ignatius Press, 1994.

Lewis, C.S. *The Complete C.S. Lewis Signature Series, The Problem of Pain,* New York, NY: HarperCollins, 2002.

Dr. Sebastian Mahfood, O.P. and Dr. Ronda Chervin, *Catholic Realism: Framework for the Refutation of Atheism and the Evangelization of Atheists*, St. Louis, MO: En Route Book & Media, 2015.

Spitzer, Fr. Robert J, *New Proofs For The Existence of God: Contributions of Contemporary Physics and Philosophy,*

Grand Rapids, MI: William, B. Eerdmans Publishing Company, 2010.

Strobel, Lee, *The Case For Christ*, Grand Rapids, MI: Harper Collins, 1998.

Wiker, Benjamin, *The Catholic Church & Science*, Charlotte, NC: TAN Books, 2011.

Woods, Thomas E, *How The Catholic Church Built Western Civilization*, Washington DC: The Eagle Publishing Company, 2005.

# Recommended Reading

*Search and Rescue: How to Bring your Family and Friends into -or back into- the Catholic Church* – by Patrick Madrid

*The Catholic Church and Science: Answering the Questions, Exposing the Myths* – by Benjamin Wiker

*Answering Atheism* – by Trent Horn

*Did Jesus Have a Last Name? And 199 Other Questions By Teenagers* – by Matthew Pinto and Jason Evert. (Also see, *Did Adam and Eve Have Belly Buttons?*)

*New Proofs For The Existence of God: Contributions of Contemporary Physics and Philosophy* – by Fr. Robert Spitzer. (A deep book using modern science)

*The Language of God: A Scientist Presents Evidence for Belief* – by Francis S. Collins (A book written by a world-class Christian scientist who even atheists respect)

*The Dawkins Delusion* – by Scott Hahn and Benjamin Wiker (A great book dismantling the New Atheism)

*The Godless Delusion: A Catholic Challenge to Modern Atheism* – by Patrick Madrid and Ken Hensley

*Catholic Realism: Framework for the Refutation of Atheism and the Evangelization of Atheists* – by Dr. Sebastian Mahfood, O.P. and Dr. Ronda Chervin.

*The Last Superstition* – by Edward Feser (A deep but incredible resource for refuting the "New Atheism" using philosophical perspectives)

*Is God a Moral Monster?* – by Paul Coplan (Answers objections to the "angry God" of the Old Testament)

*Do You Really Love Me?* – by Jason and Crystalina Evert (One of the best books on dating and relationship questions)

Made in USA - North Chelmsford, MA
1290526_9781530749188
08.27.2023 1738